MENTORING:

Leaving a Legacy

For Judy
As I remember the many "door-openers" in my life, I recognize your role as door opener & mentor for so many others in your life.
Bless you!
Lynn
Dec 2009

Lynn Smith

Mentoring: Leaving a Legacy was written initially for the German organization, *Prisca,* and was first translated and published by Brünnen-Verlag in 2007 as *Mentoring Für Frauen.*

This is the first English edition even though it was originally written in English.

Scripture quotations taken from the

HOLY BIBLE, NEW INTERNATIONAL VERSION.

National Library of Canada Cataloguing in Publication

Smith, Lynn

Mentoring: Leaving a Legacy/ Lynn Smith

ISBN 978-0-9810460-1-3

To order: Search online or contact Lynn Smith lynn@smithhouse.ca

Picture page vii by "Photomosaic (R) by Robert Silvers." www.photomosaic.com

MENTORING: LEAVING A LEGACY

Dedication

This book is dedicated to the multitude of incredible men and women whose lives have influenced mine. You have been my mentors – sometimes knowingly and intentionally - but most often without any idea that your words of affirmation and encouragement were life-giving or that your example of integrity, creativity, faith, compassion, excellence, generosity or some other admirable trait became the standard I set for myself. However well or poorly I reflect your "faces" in my life (see picture page ix) I am deeply grateful for your teaching and your influence.

PREFACE

At the conclusion of their conference on mentoring, the leaders of *Prisca*[1] asked if they could publish my teaching materials. Had I considered myself an author, I am sure I would have jumped at the opportunity. My response, however, was that I would have to do two things: get the permission of the author whose materials I was using as the framework for my teaching; and pray about it. That sounded very spiritual but in reality it was a way of opting out. I wanted to say, "No. God isn't calling me to do this," but that would have seemed presumptuous for me to declare when it was obvious I hadn't asked God.

I wasn't enthusiastic about writing a book – even a small one. First, my self identity is "teacher" not author. In my thinking, an author creates new concepts. As a teacher I simply glean information from other people, distill it for myself, and then structure it in a way that makes it applicable to others. In the case of mentoring, the whole core of my approach is based on the Stages of Power developed by Janet Hagberg in her book *Real Power*. She was an "author."

But, I said I would pray about it, and eventually I did. Then I received three phone calls within a week. The first was a request to teach a student leadership session at the college where I had worked. The topic? Mentoring. The next day, I was asked to become a mentor for the Executive Arrow Leadership program for leaders of Christian organizations in Canada. Two days later, I was asked to join a team working on implementing a mentoring program for new pastors in our denomination. By this time, I was saying, "Okay, okay, God, I get the message! I'll make the phone call to Janet Hagberg."

I really hoped that I could either persuade her to write the book, or failing that, to discover that her copyright would prevent me from using her material.

---

[1]*Prisca* is an organization in Germany which holds an annual leadership conference for women who work in Christian organizations and congregations.

It was then than I had the delightful surprise of discovering that the person who wrote the book which had given me my framework for mentoring was herself a mentor – one who shares her power - one who leaves a legacy by building into others.

Her response was an enthusiastic, "Of course you can use the material. Just indicate how people can get access to my books and website. I'm delighted that you've made an application to mentoring. How can I help you?"

Throughout the writing, I made use of her website and her network. She prayed for me, checked up on me periodically and read the manuscript to ensure that I have represented her concepts correctly.

How wonderful to see someone genuinely model the kind of empowering mentoring that characterizes my vision for mentoring.

And so, in response to God's call and with Janet's encouragement, my journey of writing began. The next surprise was how difficult it was. As I reflected on why it was so different from teaching, I came to understand the distinct advantage there is in having your audience in front of you. When I am presenting at a conference I know who is attending - I can see their faces and read their body language. I can tell when I need to clarify something and I can give personal illustrations that require voice inflections or body language to come alive. Their questions let me know what needs further exploration and explanation.

But here, in this book, I am giving information to you, the reader, without knowing who you are. I do not have the opportunity of interaction to know where I have been confusing, or where I have belaboured something that is obvious to you. And I miss having the feedback that lets me know if I have connected.

However, I have persisted because I am convinced that we need to strengthen our faith communities – making them a safe place for growth to be nurtured – and I see mentoring as the process that best incorporates all the instructions given to the early church for the maturing of its members. I am also convinced that Christ-followers need to have a greater impact as salt and light in the workplace – influencing decisions in the political, business and professional fields.

I have structured the book to answer the what, why, who, how and when questions of mentoring for both mentor and mentee. Chapter 1 identifies different types of mentoring; Chapter 2 builds a rationale for why we ought to mentor; Chapter 3 outlines what characteristics are needed to be a mentor and what to look for in a mentor for yourself; Chapter 4 gives some helpful tools for building your confidence and improving your effectiveness as a mentor; Chapter 5 is an encouragement to get started. Although the Bible doesn't use the term "mentoring," we all know that Jesus mentored his disciples. The concluding chapter looks at Jesus as our model, not to discover the techniques he used, but rather the foundational values which formed the basis of his interactions and instructions.

Some of you reading this book may already be intentional about mentoring and simply want to make the process more effective.

Some of you will be wondering how to find a good mentor.

Some of you are ready to invest in the lives of others and wonder how to be wise in choosing mentees.

Some of you may be wondering how to know if growth is actually taking place.

Some of you may just be curious about this whole mentoring business.

I am trusting that you will take what is useful and skim over what you already know; and if in the reading, you are challenged to make mentoring an intentional part of your life – as mentor and as mentee - my book will have served its purpose.

My hope is that you will find it practical and that the Stages of Power will provide a framework to guide the process.

A final word of explanation:

The desire of *Prisca* was to have a practical guide with tools and resources for Christian women to help them become life-long learners and strong committed mentors of others. I have, therefore, used female pronouns throughout and have addressed the specific strengths of women. Although women are the intended focus, I believe that men will also find the material and the approach beneficial. In many instances men are confused about how to mentor in the changing world where men and women now work side by side in the market place as well as in the church. This book may be just what they need. As my introduction indicates, men have been the primary "door openers" for me throughout my life and I wish to acknowledge, with gratitude, their significant influence.

INTRODUCTION

Change is Inevitable: Growth is Intentional.

Today's marketplace studies point to being mentored as the number one predictor of a successful career. They reveal that, "Behind every great leader is a great mentor." Actually – it's usually a number of great mentors!

Mentors are the ones who come alongside us to assist in our growth process – helping us achieve the life skills and character traits we need to reach the maturity that God intends for us.

Most of us have not had formal mentors, but like the picture of this woman, our faces reflect the multitude of faces we have encountered over the years – people who have influenced us in a variety of ways.

Some have been critics but many have been mentors who have challenged us to grow even though they may not have done so intentionally or realized their full impact at the time.

In my life, those faces would include both men and women too numerous to mention. There are a few of those, however, whose picture would be larger and brighter than most.

My mother is one. My mother grew up on a farm and determined that she would never marry a farmer and live the kind of arduous life her mother endured. She married my father, a bank clerk, and all was well – until the Great Depression came and they ended up back on the farm in order to have food to eat. The winters were particularly hard in a small drafty farmhouse. I arrived one May - just as the flowers were beginning to blossom and my mother tells me my birth was a promise of Spring to her and that she was determined to give me a better life.

She did. I have had a wonderful life – full and rich - not so much in material things as in adventures and opportunities. By the time I was 11 years old, I had lived in 13 different places as my parents followed opportunities for work, but I didn't know we were poor. I had family. And every move was another adventure.

And that has continued to be the pattern of my life. I have been blessed with opportunity after opportunity - none of which I sought or aspired to in any way. I simply stepped into new things as the opportunities presented themselves.

> ***The number one indicator of success for a child is a good relationship with a nurturing adult.***
> ***-- Fortune Magazine***

The number one indicator of success for a child is a good relationship with a nurturing adult. And that I had. My mother gave me the message that curiosity was a good thing. She encouraged my reading. As my first-grade teacher, she gave me the incredible gift of school being fun. She gave me the message that I could try anything so I learned that risk-taking was okay.

My teachers - both male and female - throughout my school years, gave me the message that I could achieve. It was a teacher who recommended me for my first job at a radio station. When I decided to go to teacher's college a year later, a male teacher loaned me the money. A university professor suggested I mark English essays which opened another whole world to me.

It was when a man in our church purchased a set of handbells for my youth choir that I first sought out a mentor. I asked the leader of another handbell choir if I could attend his practices to learn and he willingly taught me all I could grasp.

It was a man who suggested I teach religious studies in a college which is what led me to consider seminary.

It was a man who invited me to be his assistant at the seminary which led to my becoming the Dean of Students and Vice President of Student Development.

It was a man who invited me to attend the World Evangelical Fellowship in Manila which is what led me to the connections with women around the world who have enriched my life beyond measure.

Men have clearly been the door openers for me. But as for mentoring - the learning and the growth that resulted - that has mostly been with women. It was almost as if the men opened the door and I, without really knowing what I was doing, walked through seizing the opportunity for another adventure. But then I was on my own.

Fortunately my early training by my mother gave me the ability to ask questions. Reading gave me the resources for gathering information and my natural ability to teach meant I could make that information coherent for myself as well as for others.

But it was always in the context of my female relationships that I was able to process the learning and utilize it.

Once, a group of 8 women met in my house every week over a period of 3 years. We worked our way through books and Bible studies, prayed and held one another accountable.

In another city, I had a telephone friend. We would connect after the children were off to school and grapple with what a particular passage of Scripture meant for us in our daily lives.

Today I have a friend I see infrequently, but we have great conversations and prayer times on the telephone and I am blessed to have a woman as spiritual director.

So in my life, although there were very few who formally took me under their wing to guide me - it was in the context of conversations with women - either one on one - or in a group - that I gained strength, confidence, insight, wisdom, and found a safe place to be myself, develop skills and grow spiritually.

Books have also been an important source of learning for me so I include in my list of mentors a host of authors. Many people make good use of libraries, but I have always needed to buy books because I underline, highlight and write notes in the margins. Then when I go back to them I can find quickly the things I want to remember. Books are a tool for me to use.

In every opportunity, there is a risk of falling on our faces. Something that is quite important to remember as we experience the not-so-good times that we're inclined to call failures - is that there are no failures - only opportunities to grow. The only failure is the failure to learn from something. The only failure when we fall down is the failure to get up again.

I love to use the illustration of a child here when we are learning something new and difficult. I have vivid memories of my elder son learning to walk. We were celebrating his 1st Birthday. Inside the house, he was happy to crawl. But it was July and hot and we went outside on the lawn. He was wearing only a diaper and the grass tickled his bare tummy. Suddenly he stood up and walked - staggered actually - fell - stood up again - fell - a dozen times or more. As we watched, no one ridiculed the fact that he fell - but everyone cheered when he stood up again. Falling was just part of learning to walk - a perfectly natural part of the process. And the inner drive to walk was strong enough that he kept getting back up.

Isn't that how life should be? Shouldn't we all recognize that falling is a natural part of the process of growth and learning - and cheer when we get up again.

Unfortunately, our world is often full of critics when we need cheerleaders.

One young pastor, sensing a reluctance on the part of the older pastors to hand on leadership to the likes of him, stood up at a conference and said, "You're right. I don't measure up to your standards. I need more development. But I don't need you to tell me how far I've fallen short from your perspective. Don't critique me. Mentor me!"[2]

He reports that it got really quiet in the auditorium and at the end of the session a line of more than sixty pastors gathered in front of him to talk, pray and seek forgiveness.

Don't we all have that experience at sometime in our lives? We know we don't quite measure up and we feel criticized but not helped. We don't need critics – we need mentors.

We have wonderful analogies in Scripture of how we are to function as followers of Christ. The most dynamic of those is the analogy of the body – a living, growing organism – every part designed to work for the health of the whole body. Too many of us have lost the concept of living in community that was a way of life for the Hebrew people. They would have understood the body imagery more fully than we do today.

When farming families were multi-generational the wisdom of the elders was passed on to the young. Mentoring was a normal part of family and vocational life. Children worked alongside parents, learning what was expected of them in terms of responsibilities and character. In the artisan guilds, apprentices lived with their teachers in community, not just learning a skill, but also a way of life that accompanied that trade.

Today in Western countries, where many families live in urban settings, the generations are often isolated and the wisdom gained through life experience is too often lost. Older people do not have the freedom to interact with younger members of their own family and, unless specifically invited, would not feel right about guiding someone else's child. Add to that the shift from communal to individualistic values and the whole concept of mentoring has been lost.

---

[2] Martin Sanders, *The Power of Mentoring*, Christian Publishing, Camp Hill, PA, 2004, p. 15

Consequently, there is a gap – a gap which is now being felt. Men and women alike recognize that they often face the challenges of life, faith and work without adequate resources. The result is that formal mentoring and coaching has now become very popular.

While my experience illustrates the reality that a great deal of mentoring takes place informally in our daily interactions with people, my challenge in this book is to encourage readers to make it an intentional pattern of living.

The law of nature requires that we feed ourselves good food in order to have healthy bodies. The same is true of our faith communities. If we, as the body of Christ, are to have the health and vitality required to do the work of Christ in our world, we need to be intentional about recovering the communal "feeding" of one another. It is not enough to be diligent about our private devotions, to enjoy one another's company and gather for worship on Sundays unless we also connect with each other at a deep enough level to actually influence each other. We are to build each other up until we all reach maturity in Christ. This is our Biblical mandate.

Mentoring is a way of achieving that. Being intentional about it means that it will happen.

CHAPTER 1 What?

What is Mentoring?

A. Definition

The term mentor comes from Greek mythology and can be traced back to the writings of Homer almost 3000 years ago. Mentor was the "wise and trusted counselor" whom Odysseus left in charge of his household during his travels. His responsibilities included the tutoring of Odysseus's son, Telemachus.

> ***Mentor took the floor, Odysseus' friend-in-arms to whom the king, sailing off to Troy, committed his household, ordering one and all to obey the old man, and he would keep things steadfast and secure.***
> ***-- Odyssey 2.250-54***

Thus a mentor is someone assigned as tutor of another. Webster's dictionary defines it this way: "A wise and trusted teacher, guide, and friend; an elderly mentor or advisor."

In business and academic sectors, mentoring is described as the process by which an experienced person provides advice, support and encouragement to a less experienced person. In spiritual terms, mentoring is a relationship in which one person enables another to maximize the grace of God in her/his life and service. It has a sound biblical and theological basis with Jesus being the ultimate model. Christ was confidante, leader and teacher to his followers. He loved them, encouraged them, lived with them and challenged them to grow deeper in their faith and in their relationship with him and then commissioned them to establish his church.

Throughout Paul's writings to the early churches, he pleads with believers to build one another up. The list of "one another" passages is instructive.

- Serve one another — Gal 5:13
- Accept one another — Rom 15:7
- Forgive one another — Col 3:13
- Greet one another — Rom 16:16
- Bear one another's burdens — Gal 6:2
- Be devoted to one another — Rom 12:10
- Honour one another — Rom 12:10
- Teach one another — Rom 15:14
- Submit to one another — Eph 5:21
- Encourage one another — 1 Thess 5:11

Today, the term mentoring is used to describe a variety of styles of interaction, all of them involving a relationship that is nurturing – that assists in the growth of another person – and then, not surprisingly, results in the growth of the mentor as well.

There are many ways of describing a mentor: teacher, advisor, guide, counsellor, consultant, confidante, tutor, trainer, instructor, leader, conductor, director, chaperone, master, educator, loyal friend, coach or role model; but foundationally mentoring always involves a

relational process
of
sharing resources
to
empower others.

Relationships are foundational to mentoring. Note, too, that it is a process. Mentoring is a journey of walking with another person through their life experiences, helping them to reflect, find meaning and direction for the next phase of the journey.

The resources include anything that a mentor has gained through life experience: wisdom, knowledge, contacts, information, insights, confidence and perspective. And in certain situations, it could include finances.

It is important to recognize that the resources available to be shared will be different for each mentor. Figure 1 shows how the focus of each relationship is determined by assessing the needs of the mentee and the resources of the mentor. It helps to answer the questions:

- What do I need from a mentor?
- What do I have to give to a mentee?

Types of Mentoring	**Focus** *Input - depends on the skill of the mentor*	**Result** *Outcome - depends on willingness of mentee to learn*
Coaching	Skills/competence	Improve skills/competence
Discipling	Behaviour	Change in life style
Teaching	Thinking/ Information	Increase in knowledge
Counselling	Issues/Problems	Greater emotional maturity
Spiritual Direction	Relationship with God	Deeper spiritual maturity
Sponsor	Career guidance	Career advancement
Model	Specific focus will be determined by mentee: i.e. professional appearance, a skill or character trait	Determined by mentee

Figure 1

The goal of mentoring is to empower others. By empowering others, mentors are actually creating pathways for future leaders by teaching them to solve their own problems. We can come alongside another person and be a problem solver or a pathway creator. If all we do is solve problems then we have confined our followers to our own storehouse of knowledge. If we teach people to think for themselves then we are creating pathways for their future success.

B. Focus of Mentoring

There are many aspects to mentoring. Although every mentoring relationship will involve most, if not all, of the following categories at some point, it is helpful to identify the various components in order to clarify what the special need of the mentee is and what specific strengths the mentor brings to the relationship.

Coaching

If a mentee wants to improve a skill, the focus will primarily be coaching and the skill of the mentor in that specific area will be crucial. The sports analogy is clear in the use of this term; however, we often need coaching in other areas – such as leading a meeting, writing a report or answering a telephone according to the standards of the company.

Coaching a person means having a set standard to achieve. That standard may be set externally by her employer or it could be her own desire to increase her competency in an area.

In either case, the mentor and the mentee both know what the standard is and together will determine what steps are required to become more proficient. The role of the coach is to teach, encourage and support the mentee as she progresses and to celebrate small steps along the way.

Discipling

If the desired outcome is a change in life-style, the mentor will want to focus on the mentee's behaviour through a process of discipleship. The result will be moving toward Christlike behaviour. The interaction will be very similar to that of the coaching relationship, but the focus will be on values and a predetermined change in behaviour rather than increased skill.

The evaluation will naturally be more subjective than when dealing with the acquisition of a skill. The time commitment will be longer but the same steps will be followed. Set the standard together, support and encourage the small steps and then celebrate each achievement.

Teaching

Teaching is foundational to all types of mentoring. We normally think of teaching as limited to a specific subject area such as mathematical skills or learning a new language but mentoring also involves the sharing of knowledge that has been gleaned through the mentor's own life experiences.

Regardless of the focus of mentoring, there will always be some teaching involved – the passing on of information.

Counselling

At times, a mentee may get stuck in her process of maturing. This will become evident when there are inconsistencies between her values and her behaviour that neither discipling nor coaching seems to address – where no progress is being made. If a person says that punctuality is important to them but they are consistently late for meetings, there may be underlying issues that need to be uncovered and dealt with. Problems such as lack of self-esteem or lack of confidence may need to be identified and addressed before there can be further progress.

It is important, however, for the mentor to understand her own limitations and recognize when a mentee needs to be referred to a professional counsellor.

Spiritual Direction

This area of mentoring deals with a person's relationship with God and the desired outcome is a deeper spiritual maturity. Spiritual direction differs from discipleship in that discipleship places more emphasis on behaviour - having a Christlike lifestyle - whereas spiritual direction will be primarily focused on the deepening of one's relationship with Christ. This requires that the mentor herself have a vibrant relationship with God and be willing to allow the mentee the freedom to develop her own unique way of relating to God rather than becoming a clone of herself.

Sponsoring

This is the category in which financial resources may become part of the process. A mentor may see potential in the mentee in specific areas and offer to help finance training to develop that area. However, the more normal way to sponsor someone is to be a "door opener" for them. By seeing the potential in another person and offering to include them in a project or by introducing your mentee to one of your colleagues who has other resources to offer, you are giving them the benefit of your influence and your network. The focus of a sponsor is usually in the area of career development, but is not limited to that.

As described in the introduction, I have personally been the benefactor of numerous "door openers" in my life.

All of the above types of mentoring require a relationship, the closeness of which will differ depending on the focus of your interaction. In each of these, the outcome will depend on both the quality of the input of the mentor and the level of commitment to growth on the part of the mentee.

Model

There is one final type of mentoring which contradicts the definition of mentoring as a relationship. Often we will hear people name as a mentor someone whom they have not met. They may have observed or read about them, or read one of their books and been changed – empowered in some way. That person may have no knowledge of the impact they have had on another.

I watched someone who could always make at least one positive comment about whatever someone did: "That was a well-crafted presentation." "You spoke clearly." "I appreciated your appropriate use of humour." That person unknowingly became a model for me that I have tried – not always successfully - to emulate.

And we have all had the experience of having a sentence jump out of conversations, presentations or books that has stayed with us. One such sentence stands out for me from a sermon I heard many years ago: "Every encounter with another person invites them to live or to die by the way we interact with them." I have repeated that over and over again as I have counseled others in their relationships.

Another comment influenced my own involvement in leadership: "It is a sin to have a gift and not use it!!" That one sentence was like a thunder bolt that woke me up and stirred me to action on behalf of the many gifted women I saw who believed they could not exercise their leadership gifts because they were women.

We might call this unintentional or passive mentoring since there was no relationship involved. However, the normal use of the term mentoring is something we do actively and intentionally and in relationships.

Jesus, the master mentor, modeled all these types of mentoring. We are well aware of his ability to teach truths in ways that people could understand. Teaching was a part of all his interactions, but the focus varied. For example, he discipled by challenging the behaviour of his followers to make it consistent with the values that he was teaching. He became a sponsor in his interaction with Mary whose normal role would have been to help in the kitchen duties. Instead he opened the door for her to become a true learner – to sit at the feet of the teacher. His teaching became counseling with the Samaritan woman as he addressed the sin in her life and then became spiritual formation as he led her into a deeper understanding of her faith and consequently into a relationship with himself. When he sent the disciples out two by two with instructions and then debriefed them following their experience, he was doing what we could call coaching today. And of course, he was a model for all.

Purpose in separating the various types of mentoring

Identifying the various types of mentoring is not intended to communicate that a mentoring relationship will only focus on one type to the exclusion of the others. Indeed, they are intertwined. There will be teaching involved in almost all the other types. There will likely be some discipling involved in spiritual direction and vice versa. Sponsoring may be needed in a teaching focus. Issues that arise, such as anger management or time management, may include all the areas of teaching, coaching, counseling, discipling, and spiritual formation.

Understanding the distinctions, however, is helpful.

- It brings clarity.

  The word mentoring means different things to different people. The point of identifying the various components of mentoring and separating them into a chart is to avoid the confusion and disappointment of a mentee seeking one focus and a mentor expecting the focus to be something else. If a mentee needs coaching in a specific skill and the mentor thinks she's looking for spiritual direction or discipleship, expectations won't be met. If she is expecting a sponsor but the mentor is prepared to coach a skill, the relationship is doomed to failure – not because either person was wrong in their expectations, but because they were not clarified.

  The chart will help to clarify the needs at the beginning of the relationship and help to change the focus, when appropriate, during the time spent together.

- It makes for a better match.

  When seeking a mentor, it is unwise to expect one person to possess all of these strengths. A better way is to think of multiple-mentors and ask for their help in a specific area. For example, you might say, "I have observed and appreciate your ability to convey your ideas succinctly, and I would like to learn that from you. Would you consider helping me in that area?" Or it might be that you want to learn to lead a meeting well, handle conflict well, or speak up with confidence. Be as specific as you can.

- It celebrates strengths.

  It is also helpful for a mentor to understand her specific strengths so that when asked she can be specific about what she can offer and not think that she needs to be all things to her mentee.

A mentor who is able to identify and celebrate her own strengths is more likely to identify and affirm and celebrate the gifts in another. This is a strengths-based approach.

Mentoring is simply the process of coming alongside someone to assist in their growth toward the maturity that God intends for us all. A mentor is not the problem solver, but the person who assists the mentee to find the solution. Mentors provide perspective in the process of reflecting on a task or experience. The challenge for us is to become more intentional and more effective in how we do that.

CHAPTER 2 Why?

Why is Mentoring Important?

A. The Value of Mentoring

I received the following e-mail from a woman who attended a teaching session on mentoring. The capitals were hers – as if she were shouting out the message!!

Mentoring is a valuable personal practice

"YOU ARE SO RIGHT. MENTORING IS ABSOLUTELY ONE OF THE MOST SIGNIFICANT COMPONENTS OF LEADERSHIP DEVELOPMENT FOR WOMEN. IF IT WERE NOT FOR MY MENTOR I KNOW I WOULD STILL BE WALKING AROUND THAT SAME OLD MOUNTAIN OUT THERE IN THE WILDERNESS."

The truth is that we don't want to be left wandering around the same old mountain out there in the wilderness and often we need others to help us find the right path. Mentors can do that.

But mentoring isn't just for helping others find the right path, nor is it just a current fad. Although the term mentoring is not used in Scripture, the concept of mentoring is a biblical mandate for growth – both personal and corporate.

Mentoring is a biblical mandate

Paul's message to us is this:
It was [the Holy Spirit] who gave some to be apostles, some to be prophets, some to be evangelists, and some to be pastors and

teachers to prepare God's people for works of service, so that the whole body of Christ may be built up until we all reach unity in the faith and in the knowledge of the Son of God and become mature, attaining to the whole measure of the fullness of Christ" (Ephesians 4:11-13 NIV).

The whole point of giving spiritual gifts to believers was so that the body of Christ would become mature. We are to use our gifts to help one another be transformed - grow to maturity.

> ***You are successful as a leader when you leave an area a better place than when you found it. To do that best, you must leave behind people who are well equipped – with both the conviction and the will to carry on.***
> ***~ Laura Chamberlain***

The reason the word "mentoring" has become popular recently is because the old pattern of apprenticing, running family businesses and living in biblical community has given way to individualism and we are suffering because of it.

In times past, an apprentice lived with a guild master craftsman. Disciples lived with their teachers. Farms and businesses were often run by the whole family. Mentoring, in the full sense of the word, just happened. Trade skills, life skills and character development were all part of the communal living arrangement. We have lost the sense of community that used to be the norm and, along with it, the kind of mentoring that encompasses all of life.

Although we may not be able to duplicate the previous circumstances in which mentoring took place, we can make an intentional return to a communal sense of responsibility and the development of character. We can be intentional about developing mentoring relationships.

Research clearly indicates that two of the most important elements of leadership development are leadership opportunities and coaching/mentoring, especially when linked together.

This requires intentionality. Leaders who are already stretched often find it difficult to make mentoring a priority but effective leaders leave a legacy by investing themselves in the development of potential leaders. They help them develop the skills and character qualities to lead with integrity.

Since the purpose of mentoring is not just to pass on information but to be engaged in a transformational process which encompasses the personal, organizational and spiritual, mentoring can seem very nebulous. It helps, therefore, to have the various types of mentoring outlined in order to clarify the specific needs of the mentee and the strengths of the mentor as discussed in Chapter 1.

B. The Vision for Mentoring

Each of us is on a journey toward maturity. Mentoring - whether we are focused on teaching, discipling, spiritual direction, coaching, or sponsoring - has as its purpose bringing others along on that journey, helping them to grow and develop in any one or all of those spheres.

Throughout our lives we are constantly changing.

We know that change is inevitable, but if change is to result in growth, there needs to be intentionality. The question that emerges, then, is:

"What does intentional growth look like and how do we focus our mentoring relationships to be most effective for ourselves and for others?"

> ***Change is inevitable but growth is intentional.***

While everyone's journey is unique there are certain stages that are common to all of us. Research has shown that we all progress through a series of stages in the development of our identity, our use of power, and our faith journey. We need to reach a certain stage before we are motivated to consistently reach out and help others progress in their journey.

C. The Journey of Mentoring: Hagberg's Stage Theory

A very helpful framework comes from Janet Hagberg in her books, *Stages of Power*[3] which delineates the stages through which we progress in the development of personal power and *The Critical Journey*[4], co-authored with Robert Guelich, which describes a similar six stage progression in the journey of faith.

These books offer a structure which allows us to identify the stage we are in, the characteristics of that stage, the things that keep us from moving and the catalyst that pushes us toward the next stage. It helps us know where we are, where we are headed and how to identify the specific needs along the way.

By understanding mentoring through this framework of developmental stages, we can determine what needs exist and then intentionally create a process that engages the strengths of the mentee to meet those needs and that follows her natural development.

Power often has a negative connotation because of the fact that it is so often abused, but power is a God-given attribute inherent in our very being. We are created in the image of God, imbued with power to make a difference in our world. We are important. We matter. We influence our world just by the fact of our presence. The full understanding of that reality, however, is something that we learn gradually. The failure to realize that we are significant, not just for what we do but for who we are, is one of the reasons people abuse power. People who feel insignificant and powerless often resort to acts of aggression in an attempt to feel powerful.

Hagberg's explanation of the development of our real power is instructive. The theory she presents in *Real Power* is that, as we pass through various stages in our discovery of power, we move from finding our power outside of ourselves – in other people or in our achievements – to the discovery that our power is internal. At that

---

[3] Janet O. Hagberg, *Real Power: Stages of Power in Organizations*, third edition, Sheffield Publishing Company, Salem, WI, 2003 See also www.janethagberg.com

[4] Janet O. Hagberg and Robert A. Guelich, *The Critical Journey*, Sheffield Publishing Company, Salem, WI, 2005

point we no longer need to hold on to power and are free to share it – to empower others.

> ***Mentors share power***

Not everyone comes to the place of knowing that power is within them rather than something external; that it is infinite and therefore can be shared freely. Those who do are the natural mentors.

The ordered steps in our development of personal power provide a structure and a focus to mentoring which facilitates the movement through those stages (Figure 2).

My vision for mentoring is to see everyone being intentionally mentored by someone who is at least one stage ahead of them, creating a chain of mentors, with the goal of everyone reaching the stage where they are able to let go of their own need for power in order to empower others.

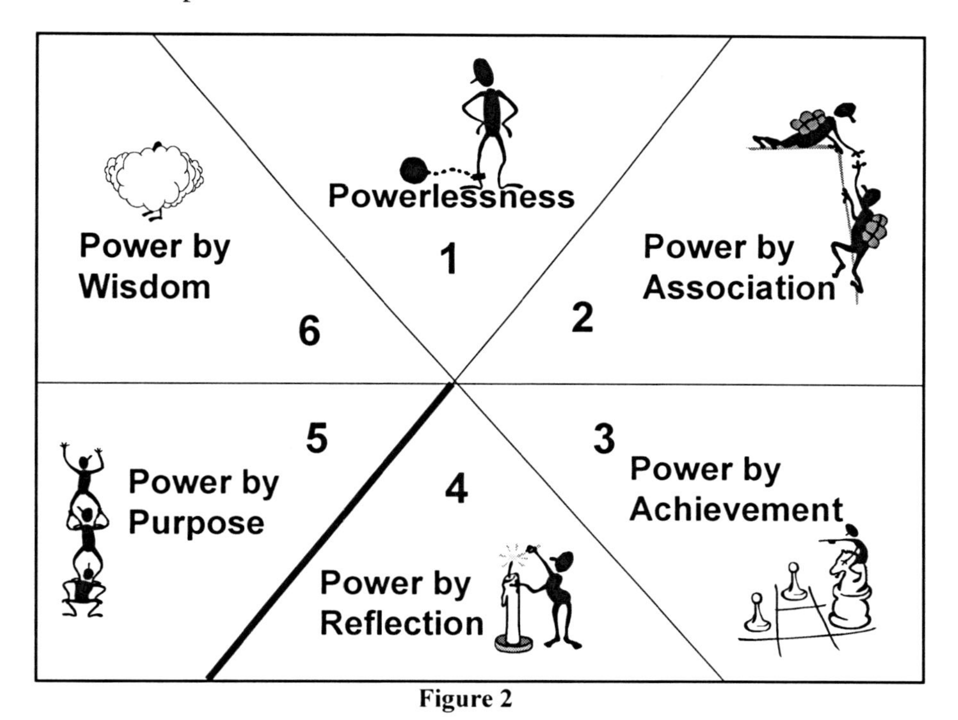

Figure 2

The Stages of Power	The Stages of Faith
Powerlessness	Discovering God
Power by Association	Learning about God
Power by Achievement	Working for God
Power by Reflection	Rediscovering God
Power by Purpose	Surrendering to God
Power by Wisdom	Reflecting God

We may be in different stages in different environments or with different people; however, we all have a home stage out of which we normally function and to which we return quickly whenever a new situation or crisis causes us to retreat to an earlier stage. As we progress through the stages we carry with us the strengths developed in the earlier stages.

It is important to note that no stage is wrong. Just as our physical development progressed through stages, so too does our development of personal power. A child who runs is not a better person or more loved than the child who is still crawling. The child has simply developed a higher level of physical functioning and we applaud each step of growth. Likewise, a person who is in Stage 3 and finds her sense of power from her achievement is not a better person than the one who in Stage 2 is getting her sense of power from the community to which she belongs. Nor is she more loved. And it is important to recognize that, although our relationship with God deepens as we mature in our faith, a person at every stage has equal access to God and is equally loved by God.

What we are looking for in our mentoring process, just as we look for it in the physical realm, is development. When a child fails to progress physically from crawling to walking to running, we become concerned and seek to discover the barrier. Just so, if we see a failure to develop in ourselves or those we mentor, we look for the factors that are hindering further growth.

There is no rule about how long we may spend in each stage; that is very individual. We can, however, become stuck or "caged" in any stage for a variety of reasons. When that happens, mentoring is especially critical. The best way to move from one stage to the next is by being mentored by someone who is operating firmly from at least the next stage.

The order of the stages is important. Again the comparison to physical development helps clarify the fact that we do not move from Stage 2 to 5 without progressing through Stages 3 and 4 any more than a child learns to skip rope before learning to stand.

The following is a brief overview of the stages including beliefs and feelings associated with each stage which will help clarify the characteristics of the various stages. To pursue this in greater detail, or for further resources, consult Janet Hagberg's website listed in the bibliography.

Stage One: Powerlessness (Discovering God)

Characteristics

The characteristics of the Stage of Powerlessness are dependency, low self-esteem, helplessness, fearfulness, a feeling of being trapped or victimized. The tendency is to think of ourselves by focusing on deficiencies: Who I am *not*!

Identity: Focus is on who I am not!

Beliefs and Feelings

- I feel powerless.
- I frequently question my self worth.
- I feel that I have to coax people to get what I want or need.
- I feel that nothing I do will make a difference in bettering my life.
- I am afraid to take risks.
- I prefer to have someone else make decisions for me.
- I seem to make poor decisions.
- Fear often immobilizes me.

Caged

We can become trapped in this stage by a sense of worthlessness, spiritual bankruptcy, martyrdom, ignorance, fear and mistrust or disapproval.

Crises or added responsibility can send us back to this stage temporarily; however, once we have the strengths of other stages, we will be able to return quickly to our home stage.

Leadership at Stage 1

When we function out of this stage in positions of leadership, our fears will make us prone to lead by force and/or manipulation which, in turn, instills fear in our followers.

Journey of Faith

Stage 1 is also the beginning of the Journey of Faith when we first discover God – either through a deep need or a sense of awe.

- I experience God by awe, a sense of need, in nature, or a search for greater meaning.
- I feel God strongly in my life.
- I feel unworthy of God's love.
- I am just beginning my journey of faith.
- God has rescued me.

Mentoring to move to Stage 2

To move from Stage 1 to Stage 2 we need to develop self-worth – to begin to discover what we have to offer rather than focusing on what we are lacking. Becoming part of a strong group or finding a strong leader to follow facilitates this move.

Mentoring at this stage would involve coaching for skills development and counseling for self-esteem and overcoming fear.

> *Betty* was stuck in Stage 1 and she was decidedly unhappy. Having been told so many times as a child that she was*

worthless and unlovable, she believed it must be true. She was unhappy in her job but couldn't risk quitting. How could she find another job? She wanted to be married but every relationship ended – reinforcing her belief that she was unlovable. She genuinely believed that she was powerless to change anything, and refused to take responsibility for her actions, attitudes or beliefs, always waiting for someone else to give her what she wanted.

Fortunately, she was befriended by a woman who, seeing her potential, began to invest in her. Mentoring for her took a variety of forms: counseling to develop self worth and find her identity in God; encouragement to develop new skills; and opportunities to build confidence in the abilities she already had.

Gradually she realized she didn't have to passively remain a victim. She discovered she had something of value to contribute to others and could ask for what she needed rather than expect others to rescue her.

Today, she is participating in a healthy community where her gifts are being used and she is beginning to blossom.

**name changed*

Stage Two: Power by Association (Learning about God)

Characteristics

The characteristics of a person in the Power by Association stage are dependency on other people perceived to be powerful, learning and conforming to the culture, gaining self-awareness, apprenticing and needing to belong.

> ***Identity: Focus is on who others say I am.***

In this stage we find meaning and identity from the group to which we belong. Answers are found in the leader, the cause or the belief system. This is a comfortable place to be and many of us stay here for a considerable period of time. We learn the communal language, values and practices – the way to behave in order to be included and not ostracized by the group. It is others who give us a sense of power and it is belonging that gives us meaning. Therefore, our focus is no longer on our deficiencies but on how others perceive us. The community tells us who we are.

Beliefs and Feelings

- I feel that I have to prove myself.
- I am "learning the ropes."
- I seek information and advice from as many people as possible.
- I am intensely loyal to my boss.
- I consciously imitate other people's behaviour.
- My self-concept is dependent on what others say about me.
- I am easily influenced by those I perceive to be more powerful.
- I have difficulty making decisions.
- I am just beginning to discover and develop my skills.
- I sometimes feel naïve.
- I feel stuck in my job.

Caged

We get trapped in Stage 2 when we become convinced that only the group which has embraced us holds the right beliefs, has the right cause or follows the right leader.

That translates into arrogance, a "we against them" attitude that keeps us bound to live by the established rules. Other factors that keep us caged at this stage may include lack of confidence, a strong need for security, fear of success and an obsession with finding someone or something outside ourselves to make us satisfied. Another reason why women can get stuck in Stage 2 is an unwillingness on the part of their community to acknowledge their spiritual gifts and give them opportunities to develop them. This is especially true of the gift of leadership.

Leadership at Stage 2

When we hold positions of leadership with Stage 2 as our home stage, we will be excellent at following the rules and being loyal to an organization. We will influence through relationships but our insecurity will interfere with effective leadership. We will often have difficulty making decisions because we second-guess our decisions and we instill dependency in our followers because we are not secure enough to set people free to act independently.

Journey of Faith

Stage 2 in the faith journey is the stage of discipleship – the stage where we learn about God and the way to live as a believer. When we are embraced by a community of faith, we incorporate their beliefs about God and their way of living out those beliefs as our own. Our concept of God is formulated by what we are taught.

- My community makes me feel worthwhile.
- I am certain that my beliefs are right.
- I am enjoying learning about my faith.
- I like being with like-minded people.
- I have spiritual heroes and heroines.
- I am growing in my understanding of God.
- I feel comfortable knowing that I am living by the rules.

Mentoring to move to Stage 3

The movement to Stage 3 requires a beginning self confidence; therefore, we need help to develop abilities and strengths.

Teaching and coaching become the primary types of mentoring needed at this stage to develop confidence in our ability, although a sponsor can be significant as well. Mentors can be influential by giving support and encouragement in seeking challenging opportunities and new responsibilities, giving honest feedback, providing skills training and offering their network.

Good goals for a mentee in this stage would be taking risks to develop confidence, getting coaching to become competent, learning to take care of oneself and recognizing contributions.

> *Ingrid* is an example of someone who was stuck in Stage 2 by her lack of confidence. She was an alcoholic, had low self-esteem and problems in her marriage. Five years ago she discovered through mentoring that she had incredible strengths borne out of her adversity. Today she is leading a Christian recovery group and speaking in public and her demeanor has changed from one of an apologetic stance to that of a radiant daughter of the King. She is now very definitely functioning in Stage 3.*
>
> **name changed*

Stage Three: Power by Achievement (Working for God)

Characteristics

The Power by Achievement Stage is characterized by success, ambition, competitiveness, energy, competence, charisma and realism. In this stage, we place a high value on the symbols or status that come as a result of our accomplishments and we are often not aware that there is more to life than our current area of responsibility or control.

> ***Identity: Focus is on what I do.***

We may stay in Stage 3 for many years as we become more confident and competent and develop a mature ego. All cultures reward this stage in some way whether the achievement is in the area of manual labour, financial success, sports trophies, travel or fame. It is here that confidence is built.

Beliefs and Feelings

- I think power is finite – there is only so much to go around.
- Symbols such as salary, titles, material possessions and degrees are important.

- I believe power involves being in control.
- My main satisfaction comes from my work.
- I am willing to compromise personal values to succeed at work.
- I like the challenge of responsibility.
- I believe that I can earn power.
- My desire is to be successful.

Caged

We can get trapped in this stage when we see life as performance and need to hold on to control. We can become overly zealous, weary in well-doing and self-centered, often not realizing that we are stuck.

Leadership in Stage 3

Leadership in Stage 3 is focused on success strategies and we can become upset when results are not forthcoming. Our personal competence and ego are on the line and therefore we can take failure of our plans personally. We inspire a winning attitude in our followers and often guide by personal persuasion and charisma.

This is the stage of leadership most frequently found in organizations because Stage 3 leaders are the most outwardly successful.

Journey of Faith

In our faith journey, this is the stage when we are working for God and being productive in our spiritual life. We discover new gifts and take on responsibilities within our faith community with a new sense of confidence. Symbols of success may be more responsibility, a plaque of appreciation, a new challenge or just the recognition that we are making a difference. We are aware of our abilities, find opportunities to use them, and have a satisfying sense of success.

- I feel good about my gifts and wish to share them.
- I like to be recognized for the contributions I make in my faith community.

- I have achieved some of my spiritual goals.
- I get tired from doing so many things.
- I like teaching others about the faith.

Mentoring in Stage 3

Coaching is the primary type of mentoring that Stage 3 people are looking for as they move toward their goal of success. There are a multitude of skills needed for competency in any given area, and until a person has achieved a certain level of success, they will not be ready to let go and move on to Stage 4.

Mentoring to move to Stage 4

The first three stages are characterized by external power – coming from our connections or our achievements. In these stages we develop the "capacity to act" which is the usual meaning of power. When we move to stage 4, we begin to experience internal power which comes from the "capacity to reflect." We do not lose the capacity to act, which we have developed, but we act for different reasons.

Often a personal crisis is required to move because Stage 3 appears to be the pinnacle of success and it feels good to be there. The loss of a job, family problems or a health crisis can shatter the dream and bring the realization that we are not in control. There can also be a crisis of faith when we realize that "pat answers" no longer suffice or that working for God isn't as satisfying as it once was. Then we begin to look for something more lasting than symbols of achievement to give life meaning.

The process of moving from Stage 3 to Stage 4 requires a different type of mentoring. We need help to let go of the symbols of success and the need to be seen as strong, confident, perfect and competent. We need to accept the loss of certainty, accept vulnerability, deal with feelings of abandonment, find direction rather than answers, learn to be alone and reflective, build networks and concentrate on the present. This shift is difficult and cannot be forced but it can be encouraged by a caring mentor.

Specific growth goals for the mentee could include choosing to give up a specific symbol of success, developing self-reflection skills, interviewing people in Stages 4, 5 and 6, answering a number of "What would you do if?" questions, choosing a cause to champion and beginning to mentor someone else.

> *Sophie* is a bright and energetic young woman who had dreamed for many years of attaining the Vice-president position in the company she worked for. She felt she deserved it, and her boss had hinted several times that she was ready for that responsibility. So when she was called to his office, she knew what to expect. What she didn't expect was her reaction to the offer. Instead of responding as she had rehearsed many times, she hesitated. Suddenly the role didn't seem so attractive. She was confused. Why wasn't she ecstatic?*
>
> *She asked for time to think about it and immediately sought out a mentor who, with some probing questions, helped her realize that the company's values were in conflict with her own and that the status of the position was ultimately not as important to her as maintaining her internal values. She had not understood the values conflict – thinking that her dis-ease was due to not being in control, rather than the deeper issue of incongruent values.*
>
> *She actually resigned and has since started her own consulting business built on her own values. Both she and her business are flourishing.*
>
> **name changed*

Making that move from external to internal power is not something that comes automatically and at least one study[5], which involved 1,605 business and professional men and women, shows a marked gender and age difference in the various stages of power.

Home Stage by Age (Figure 3)

Age was clearly a factor – probably related to life experience. No one under the age of 21 tested beyond Stage 3. Of the participants in the 21-30 age bracket, 14% had moved to Stage 4, 29% in the 31-40 age bracket, rising to 40% of the 41-50 year olds. Then

[5] Research conducted at Augsburg College in 2000 (see www.janethagberg.com)

surprisingly, the numbers drop to 31% of the 51- 60 age bracket and back to 19% in the over 61 range.

Age	Stage 1	Stage 2	Stage 3	Stage 4	Stage 5	Stage 6
< 21	33%		66%			
21 - 30	11%	31%	44%	12%	1%	1%
31 - 40	9%	20%	51%	19%	.5%	.5%
41 - 50	9%	13%	46%	30%	.6%	.4%
51 - 60	6%	15%	48%	28%	3%	
61+	13%	8%	60%	19%		

Figure 3

Home Stage by Gender (Figure 4)

The gender differences are interesting. More women than men were in Stage 2 (19% compared to 15%) and many more men than women were in Stage 3 (61% compared to 46%). However, the number of women who moved to Stage 4 and beyond (internal power) was significantly higher than the number of men. Only 16% of the men tested had moved beyond Stage 3 compared to 26% of the women.

	Stage 1	Stage 2	Stage 3	Stage 4	Stage 5	Stage 6
Males	8%	15%	61%	15%	1%	
Females	9%	19%	46%	23%	2%	1%

Figure 4

Home Stages (Figure 5)

This study indicates that even among business and professional men and women, the majority have not progressed beyond external power – a full 77.8% are in Stages 1, 2 and 3 - meaning that fewer than 25% are living out of their internal power.

Stage	1	2	3	4	5	6
Percent	9.1	17.8	50.9	21.2	0.9	0.6

Figure 5

Stage Four: Power by Reflection (Rediscovering God)

Characteristics

Moving to Stage 4 is a significant transformation from a mentality of scarcity to one of abundance. Power is no longer finite. It comes from within and therefore cannot be taken away from us. When something is securely ours, we are free to share it with others. We can empower others without being diminished ourselves.

> ***Identity: Focus is on discovering who I am.***

The shift is from "doing" to "being" where the question of identity is no longer about what I do but about who I am. It is the beginning of the move from success to significance.

In this stage we typically are competent, confident and reflective, skilled at mentoring and comfortable with our personal style. Decisions made at this stage will be made according to personal values rather than on the basis of making someone else happy (Stage 2) or holding on to power (Stage 3). This is a time of integration of faith and work and of developing our own style.

Beliefs and Feelings

- Others are deliberately choosing me to be a mentor for them.
- I have consciously chosen to act with integrity, despite the consequences.
- It is important for me to have a personal style - not what the organization expects.
- I find that symbols of success do not motivate me the way they used to.

- I enjoy collaborating with others even though I could easily be in charge.
- I have learned to admit weaknesses and mistakes without putting myself down.
- I have been challenged to change my thinking about life and work.
- I am able to speak out when asked to compromise my values.
- I am somehow different from who I used to be.
- I no longer need to assert my independence.

Caged

It is in Stage 4 that we encounter the WALL.

Failure to move through the WALL to Stage 5 happens when we become trapped in Stage 4 by seeing no need for a life purpose, refusing to let go of ego, getting stuck in confusion or becoming obsessed with self-examination.

Leadership

It is in Stage 4 that we actually become leaders rather than just holding leadership positions. People follow us now because they choose to rather than because they must or are afraid not to. Our reputation for being fair and offering a listening ear gives influence whether or not we are in a position of authority.

Although people hold positions of leadership in stages two and three, true leadership begins at stage four. These are the people who have faced a crisis of integrity. It's not that people at stages two and three lack integrity but that, as they resolve crises in their work, the issue of integrity is not the major one they face. The goal for people at stage two is to satisfy the person they are answerable to; the goal for people at stage three is to hold on to their position of authority in order to gain their own goals.[6]

---

[6] Hagberg, *Real Power*, p. 149

In Stage 4 we are concerned with doing the right thing, the fair or just thing in the long run. We do not depend on immediate results but on maintaining quality and effectiveness. We nourish an environment that encourages others to flourish, innovate, take risks and learn about themselves without shame, genuinely caring for other people.

Self esteem is not tied to our success. We do not operate out of fear or ego gratification, nor revert to traditional authoritarian styles when things get tough, and we do not have to prove our worth by supplying all the answers.

These are the leaders who make excellent mentors.

Journey of Faith

To observers, it could appear that those of us in Stage 4 are losing our faith, when in reality we are rediscovering God at a much deeper level. In effect, God is released from the box and allowed to become Lord – taking over control. Ambiguity can be embraced; uncertainty can be tolerated. This is the place of developing discernment and surrendering my will to the will of God.

- My image of God has changed from earlier times.
- My faith has been challenged.
- I have experienced a nagging search for personal meaning.
- I am looking for direction rather than answers.
- I have lost the certainty about life that I once had.

Mentoring in Stage 4

Mentoring needs in Stage 4 involve preparing to encounter the WALL. We need questions which encourage solitude and reflection, and which invite deep thinking about being, integrity and values. We need opportunities to try things that cause a shift in thinking and encouragement to accept our vulnerability.

Mentoring goals would include facing the fear of letting go, confronting the things that are holding us back, getting spiritual direction, discovering the inconsistency between our stated values and our true values – the ones we actually live by.

The process of moving to Stage 5 requires going through the WALL. This is the place of meeting our controlling ego, often in the form of a crisis.

The crisis may be a relational loss, job loss, health issue, facing mortality, a crisis of faith. Or it may be simply reaching the pinnacle of success and finding it empty. We think we are still in control of our lives and the WALL compels us to let go.

For some, the WALL experience can last a long time – for others it is a repeated confrontation.

The WALL: A Place of Transformation

Characteristics

The WALL can be described as a place of both tremendous loss and tremendous gain, both exhilarating and painful. It takes courage to choose to go through to the unknown instead of going back to the success that we know. It takes courage to let go of our ego and embrace the process when we are not sure what the outcome will be. It is a time of moving from head to heart, letting go of control, going into our core and embracing the unwelcome parts of ourselves.

Beliefs and Feelings

- I am aware of the shadow parts of me.
- I am learning to embrace the inner me.
- I am in pain.
- I am facing my worst fears.
- I feel as if I am losing control.

Journey of Faith

People describe time in the WALL as a deep well, an abyss, a slow descent, a dark tunnel, a pit, a prison cell, a dark night or a valley.

Any one of those is true, but it is also a place of healing if we will surrender to the God who heals.

- God feels distant.
- I feel as if my will is pitted against God's.
- I am surprised by new insights.
- The old answers no longer suffice.

Caged

We can get trapped at the WALL by the desire to ward off pain, not wanting to let go of our will or lose control because we believe there is too much to lose.

Mentoring to move through the WALL to Stage 5

Moving through the WALL cannot be done by our own will – for that would mean we are still in control. The only way through the WALL is to surrender.

We need help to let go of control and self-centeredness, learn to live in community, accept God's purpose for life, be willing to commit to whatever it takes, find peace through giving up the search for self, allow for new certainty in God and be open to the cost of obedience.

Mentors can help us to:

- move beyond our intellect and become intimate with God.
- face and embrace all of self, discover our deepest desires.
- find glimpses of wisdom and light in the dark times.
- understand that pain is an opportunity for growth.
- explore our own passion, stay accountable.
- seek wholeness through personal healing.
- believe in healing before it happens.
- face fears and develop courage.
- develop discernment.

- accept ambiguity.
- find purpose.

Note: This is when we need someone who has been through the WALL herself to listen and offer support and to give safe opportunities to explore ambiguity, paradox and unknowns. We need the assurance that going through the WALL is a life transformation.

What the research shows is that the potential pool of mentors for this stage of development is fairly small (Figure 5). One solution is to team up with someone else who is facing the WALL and covenant together to share the journey.

> *This was my own experience the first time I encountered the WALL. Although I taught school prior to having children, it was while I was home with my children that I really began to develop my competence and discover an identity that came from what I was able to do (Stage 3). I was involved in church leadership, marked English essays for a university professor, led the youth choir and began a handbell choir. One symbol of achievement that meant a lot to me was the mark my handbell choir received in a music festival. The reason it was so important was that I had just learned about handbells from the leader of the other choir in the competition and we received a higher mark. It sounds so petty now but I was really proud of that achievement.*
>
> *I was beginning to discover an identity apart from my role as wife and mother. I went back to university, learned French and began to teach part time. I had a good life. Suddenly my husband was transferred across the country to a city where I knew no one. I felt like a tree which had all the branches cut off, then uprooted and transplanted in an unfamiliar place. Everything that had given me my identity was taken away and I didn't know who I was. During the hymns at church, all I could hear was the sound of the handbells playing a descant and I would fight back the tears and often beat a hasty retreat. One day a woman put her arm around my shoulder and said quietly, "It hurts to move, doesn't it?" I couldn't respond at the time without weeping, but I went to visit her that week. The result was that we gathered eight women – all of us hurting in some way - and together over the next 3 years we shared and prayed and grew and healed.*

The first step in healing was to discover that stripping away the things that I thought had given me my identity was a gift. It allowed me to discover that my identity didn't come from all the things I was doing but from my relationship with God. I realized that if I had not been forced to give up all my wonderful "working for God" achievements, as enjoyable as they were, and rediscover God at a deeper level, I would not have been ready for the next encounters at the WALL.

Although my identity was now settled, there were other walls to face – each one full of pain and confusion – but each one an incredible gift.

It was in dealing with a foster child that I faced my limitations – my inability to "fix" someone. I learned the reality of the demonic and the necessity of spiritual warfare. Facing my brokenness over my sense of failure made me surrender my "abilities" and discover that God could use a broken healer.

My husband's open heart surgery was the WALL that forced me to confront the source of my security. Was it in my relationship with my husband or my relationship with God? When I came to the place of knowing in my heart that whether my husband lived or died, he was in God's hands and whether he lived or died, I too, was in God's hands – only then did I have peace.

It was the birth of our first grandchild two months later that challenged my values. The fact that she was born with Down Syndrome forced me to face the reality that I had unknowingly absorbed the "success and self-sufficiency" values of our culture and that I needed to replace those with God's values of life and love in order to fully embrace her as God's gift to us.

Caring for my mother, who suffered from Alzheimer disease, brought me the understanding that God is vastly bigger than our illness and our intellect and even though she didn't know who or where she was much of the time, God knew her and loved her.

I can recount these lessons quickly now but the WALL experiences were neither short nor pleasant. What I do know is that God is faithful in the dark times and places and that we are transformed in the process.

If there isn't someone available who has been through the WALL to assist you in the process, then be open to a quiet invitation to join others and share the process.

I also know that Goes does not waste our WALL experiences. It is in the difficult times of life that what we know moves from our head to our heart. At the WALL – or in the valley - we gain wisdom and insight that enable us to compassionately walk with others through their walls and their valleys.

Stage Five: Power by Purpose (Surrendering to God)

Characteristics

When we allow God to take us through the WALL into Stage 5, we are transformed. We become self accepting, calm, visionary, humble, confident of our life purpose, generous in empowering others and deeply spiritual. We have a vocation or ministry and a genuine focus on others' best interests which leads us to love, serve and empower others. Life is lived in an interdependent community rather than a community that exists to tell us who we are and what we believe. In stage 2 we need our community to mirror back to us who we are. They exist for our benefit. In Stage 5, we simply see others for who they are. We live with them in mutuality. We serve others without diminishing ourselves. Consequently we do not burn out at this stage.

Identity: Focus is on empowering others in community.

We no longer borrow power from others – we can simply be with them – giving and receiving in mutuality. Our sense of identity moves beyond self to being one among others. We see others and seek to serve them.

When you find someone in Stage 5, cherish that one!

Beliefs and Feelings

- I have a life purpose that reaches beyond myself and my organization.

- I believe power is infinite – there is enough to go around.
- I have been given energy or stamina beyond my own to survive a crisis or illness.
- I have been "given" the right words or quality to be available for another.

Caged

Although we are not really stuck in Stage 5, we can appear to others to be out of touch with practical concerns and careless about "important" things.

Some of the things that can hold us back from Stage 6, where God is everything, would be lack of faith, an inability to live with ambiguity or an unwillingness to give up enough.

Leadership

Stage 5 leaders are servant leaders. Our main goal is empowering others to be more fully human and more fully satisfied. While we are essential to an organization, we may not be comfortable any more in an organization because our vision goes beyond the tangible and immediate to the intangible and the future: love, justice, peace.

Stage 5 leaders give their followers a non-critical acceptance which frees them to rise above their insecurities and fears.

Faith journey

Stage 5 is the stage of surrender to the purposes of God – a time of waiting on the Lord for the next step rather than long-range planning. Our focus is outward, but from a new grounded centre of ourselves.

- I have a glimpse of God's purpose (vocation, call, ministry) for my life.
- I am living out of a stillness at my core.
- I am able to be vulnerable and yet feel safe.
- I have the assurance that I am known by God.

- I look forward to spending time with God.
- I can serve others out of genuine love for them.
- I am comfortable being alone.
- My focus is no longer on the gifts of God, but on the presence of God.

Mentoring for moving to Stage 6

To move from Stage 5 to Stage 6, we need to become willing to live fearlessly in the face of the paradoxes of life, with deep spirituality and with the potential of losing everything for sake of something much bigger.

Mentoring goals here would be to stop striving and just evolve, grow deeper, see God in all of life, find satisfaction in vocation, find contentment in being whole and think universally.

> *Mary* is an artist who I believe is moving from Stage 5 to 6 – not because she talks about it, but because there is a humility about her that requires no accolades, no affirmation, no attention given to her at all. She lives simply and graciously, with a child-like trust in the goodness of God and of life and with a profound sense of peace. Her life story contains many "wall" experiences which she will share - but without a hint of bitterness, only gratitude for the good things that have emerged from the heartbreaks.*
>
> *Her mentor has been life itself - with God at the centre - and her journey has been expressed in her art. Her peace comes from her conviction that God is writing her story and that her role is simply to surrender and allow the story to unfold as God chooses. In the same way, her art emerges as she surrenders to the creative spirit within her and it brings contentment and satisfaction.*
>
> *To some she could appear naïve – but it's clear that her wisdom comes from having embraced the challenges of life rather than hiding from them and finding both strength and peace in the process.*
>
> **name changed*

Stage Six: Power by Wisdom (Reflecting God)

Characteristics

When we arrive at Stage 6, we are a paradox. We are at one and the same time deeply content in ourselves yet deeply disturbed by the suffering of the world. We work on issues that will relieve pain for others, yet accept our own without a sense of being a martyr. We make a strong impact but prefer not to be brought into the limelight.

Identity: Focus is reflecting God.

The power of Stage 6 is self-sacrifice, and the picture of power at this stage is a person whose power pervades the surrounding space, touching other people. These are the people who are detached from things and stress, who are unafraid of death and whose simple presence touches us in the depths of our being.

Beliefs and Feelings

- I am totally faithful to God.
- I am detached from things.
- I love my enemies.
- I would give up everything for God.
- My life is consumed by the fire of the Holy Spirit.

Not Caged

We are not caged in Stage 6. We may seem to others to be out of touch with the world, neglectful of self, too sacrificial and wasting our lives.

Leadership

In Stage 6, we don't look to lead, we just live. We have no aspiration to leadership, but rather just live out our life purpose with inner peace and wisdom. As a result, we inspire in others a confidence that there is nothing to fear and nothing to strive for.

Stages of Power Framework for Mentoring

The vision for mentoring is to see ourselves and our mentees progress from external power to internal power; from working *for* God to surrendering *to* God; from a scarcity mentality to an abundance mentality; from needing others to loving others; from holding onto power to sharing it freely. This is the process of transformation which we are called to assist.

The value of mentoring is that it provides an intentional process that fulfills our biblical mandate to build one another up, enhances any organization we belong to, and ensures that the leadership challenges of the future will be met by those who are better equipped to face them.

It takes individuals changing themselves and then acting differently wherever they are, treating people differently, asking different questions, questioning policies, working unceasingly on issues, seeing a vision and acting in everyone's best interest. It is a transformed individual who can assist in another's transformation, and together they transform organizations and countries.[7]

A mentor's purpose is to assist in the development of another person who will then assist in the development of another person - and the cycle goes on.

Summary comments

Although I have used the inclusive "we" throughout, I have done so only to be consistent, and not to indicate that I have personally moved through all the stages. In fact, the research indicates that very few ever reach Stage 6.

You can mentor or be mentored in any stage – the focus will be different at each stage; however, mentoring becomes a natural life-style in Stage 5.

The stages are very fluid. We move back and forth between them regularly.

---

[7] www.janethagberg.com

We can experience more than one stage at the same time.

Stages 1, 2 and 3 are stages of external power whereas Stages 4, 5, and 6 are stages of internal power.

People in Stages 1-3 can coach in skills, teach information, and challenge behaviour.

We take with us all the strengths from a previous stage when we move on so that Stage 5 people will still have the competencies that they developed in Stage 3. They may be doing exactly the same things – but doing them from a totally different place within themselves.

Stage 4 people are good mentors and discover that people seek them out.

Stages 4 and higher are needed for internal integrity and character issues.

Stage 5 people can't help but mentor and so they seek out others to mentor.

Stage 6 people just influence by who they are.

Understanding the stages helps me to:

- ask more specifically for the assistance I need.
- focus more effectively on another's needs.
- be more realistic about my own growth or someone else's.
- begin to ask more focused questions – questions that are stage related.
- be more intentional about the process of growth.
- determine which focus of mentoring is most needed and give that greater emphasis.

With this framework in mind, we can more easily identify the stage we are in most of the time and as we interact with others we will discover where they are as well. The question then becomes, "How do I come alongside that person?" or, "Who do I find to come alongside me?"

STAGES OF POWER

	STAGE 1	STAGE 2	STAGE 3
STAGES of POWER	**Powerlessness**	**Power by Association**	**Power by Achievement**
Leads by…	Force or manipulation	The Rules	Personal persuasion
Leaders at this Stage inspire…	Fear	Dependency	A winning attitude
Characteristics	Secure and dependent Low in self-esteem Uninformed Helpless but not hopeless	Learning the Culture Apprentices Dependent on the supervisor/ leader New self-awareness	Mature ego Realistic Competitive Expert Ambitious
Motivation to move	Self esteem Skill development	Gaining confidence Taking risks	Gaining integrity
Deterrent to move	Fear	Need for security	Need for control Not knowing you're stuck

<table>
<tr><th>STAGE 4</th><th>The WALL</th><th>STAGE 5</th><th>STAGE 6</th></tr>
<tr><td>Power by Reflection</td><td rowspan="6">The WALL is the place of trans-formation.

It requires courage.

The only way through is to surrender your will to God.

Characteristics are:
Discomfort
Surrender
Healing
Awareness
Forgiveness
Acceptance
Love
Closeness to God
Discernment
Solitude
Reflection</td><td>Power by Purpose</td><td>Power by Wisdom</td></tr>
<tr><td>Modeling integrity</td><td>Empowering others</td><td>Being wise</td></tr>
<tr><td>Hope
Inner security</td><td>Love and service</td><td>Inner peace</td></tr>
<tr><td>Reflective
Confused
Competent in collaboration
Strong
Comfortable with personal style
Skilled at mentoring
Showing true leadership</td><td>Self accepting, courageous
Calm, visionary
Humble
Generous in empowering others
Confident of life calling</td><td>Self sacrificing
Ethical
Comfortable with paradox
Unafraid of death
Quiet in service
Compassion for the world
Integrated</td></tr>
<tr><td>Letting go of ego
Facing fear</td><td>Becoming connected with the universe</td><td>Embracing spirituality fully</td></tr>
<tr><td>No life purpose
Not letting go of ego</td><td>Lack of faith, unwilling to give up enough</td><td>Human restraints</td></tr>
</table>

STAGES OF FAITH

	STAGE 1	STAGE 2	STAGE 3
FAITH JOURNEY	**Recognition of God: Discovering God**	**The Life of Discipleship: Learning about God**	**The Productive Life: Working for God**
Characteristic	Sense of awe Sense of need Natural awareness Greater meaning in life A sense of innocence	Meaning from belonging Answers found in leader, cause or belief system Sense of rightness Security in our faith	Uniqueness in the Community Responsibility Value placed on symbols A spiritual goal reached
Motivation to move	Sense of belonging Accepting self worth	Taking risks Recognize gifts/ uniqueness/ contribution	Letting go of success Accepting vulnerability
Deterrent to move	Sense of worthlessness Ignorance Martyrdom Spiritual bankruptcy	"We" against "them" Group arrogance Rigid in rules	Overly zealous Self-centered See life as performance Weary in well-doing

STAGE 4	The WALL	STAGE 5	STAGE 6
The Journey Inward: Rediscovering God	**The Wall is the place of trans-formation**	**The Journey Outward: Surrendering to God**	**The Life of Love: Reflecting God**
Search for direction not answers Loss of certainties in life and faith God released from box Apparent loss of faith	Movement is by letting go of control, embracing your shadow, going to your core, finding intimacy with God, glimpsing wisdom	New sense of horizontal life Renewed sense of God's acceptance Sense of calling, vocation or ministry Deep calm Focus on others' best interests	Christ-like living in total obedience to God Wisdom Compassion Detachment from things and stress
Accepting God's purpose for our lives Open to the cost of obedience		Seeing God in all of life Growing deeper	Life abandoned to God
Consumed by self-assessment		Out of touch with practical concerns	None. Others see an apparent waste of life/neglect of self

CHAPTER 3 Who?

Who can Mentor?

A. Characteristics of an Effective Mentor

Studies of high potential and successful leaders have found that key events (both opportunities and hardships) and other people, are the most significant factors in their development. Interaction with a variety of role models or mentors with diverse strengths, styles, and skills has been found to be most effective. Mentors can include family members, teachers, bosses and even peers.

In fact, we are all mentoring and being mentored in informal ways, if not formally, but using the word "mentoring" to describe the process scares us so we often back off just when our input is most needed and most valuable.

We often assume we have to "have it all together" in order to mentor someone else so we shy away from it. However, anyone who has been mentored will tell you that what made it significant was the time given them, the belief in them, the vulnerability and honesty shown, and the opportunity to learn not only from strengths and successes but from weaknesses and failures as well!!

Although the specific focus of mentoring will depend on the needs of the mentee as discussed in Chapter 1, and their Stage of Power as discussed in Chapter 2, there are some general characteristics of effective mentors. A mentor needs to:

- love - this communicates acceptance.
- serve - this models vulnerability and humility.
- teach - this imparts knowledge.
- confront - this challenges inconsistencies and promotes growth.
- affirm - this recognizes giftedness and strengths.
- be real - this builds trust and confidence.

Anyone who will love, serve, teach, confront, affirm and be real will be able to create a safe place that nurtures growth – and thus can be a mentor.

At different times in our lives we need a mentor whose style is that of an encourager – a grace-giver – and at other times we need an exhorter – a truth-teller.

A grace-giver acts primarily as a friend and cheerleader, giving encouraging words, making suggestions and listening well. The focus is on process. Grace-givers are a gift. We all need to be recipients of grace.

A truth-teller acts primarily as a teacher or supervisor assigning tasks, telling us what she sees, and being more concerned with the product than the process. Truth-tellers are also a gift. It is important for our growth that we have others in our lives whom we can trust to tell us the truth - people who care about us enough to speak the truth lovingly even when it is difficult.

B. Women as Mentors

Women bring strengths to situations and relationships that have often been seen as weaknesses but are in fact the very qualities that hold our society together[8] and create the environment in which growth can take place. Women tend to be strong in the areas of:

---

[8] Jean Baker Miller, *Toward a New Psychology of Women*, Beacon Press, Boston, 1976, pp. 29-48

- Vulnerability
- Connectedness
- Nurturing
- Cooperation
- Creativity

These are the qualities that make for good mentors. Women are not afraid of being vulnerable. We reach out to connect with others, find ways of cooperating and use our creativity to problem solve. Mentoring is a nurturing activity and there are many forms of mentoring to suit the varying needs of the one being mentored and the strengths of the mentor.

Recent research is showing that women react differently to stressful situations than men do. According to a UCLA study,

> men tend to isolate themselves whereas women tend to reach out for community in order to share on a deeply personal basis and nurture others. It appears that this different reaction is due to a chemical response to stress. Oxytocin, a hormone, is released which encourages her to tend children and gather with other women instead of the "fight or flight" reaction normally assumed to be the reaction to a stressful situation. Then, when women engage in this tending and befriending activity, more oxytocin is produced which further counters stress and produces a calming effect. The reason this doesn't happen for men appears to be because the hormone, testosterone, reduces the effects of oxytocin, whereas estrogen enhances it.[9]

This natural response of women to stress may explain why more women than men remain in stage 2 since that is where "befriending" is first experienced. It may also be the reason why mentoring has changed as women have moved into the business and corporate world.

The way mentoring used to work in organizations was that a senior male executive, who was several rungs higher up the ladder, would

---

[9] Quoting Drs. Shelley E. Taylor and Laura Cousino Klein, co-authors of a UCLA study on Women's Stress, "Psychological Review" 2000, pp. 411-429

identify a younger version of himself as his protégé and act as a sponsor to steer him toward career-enhancing projects or advantageous assignments. Mentoring was all about connections and chemistry between two people who had a lot in common.

Today, as women have entered the world of work, they've found that the old model of mentoring doesn't work for them. They can't rely on men to pick female mentees and they don't wish to socialize on the golf course or on a fishing trip to form personal bonds. But they do need to be able to meet together and so they have made mentoring more organized and focused. They have also extended mentoring to include more than the sponsorship represented by the corporate ladder.

Women's mentoring[10] is:

More about:	than about:
Commitment	Chemistry
Personal growth	Promotion
Development	Favouritism
Learning	Power
Cultivating uniqueness	Creating a clone

Recognizing the strengths women bring to mentoring is not to negate the value of having both men and women among your mentors. Look to the qualities rather than the gender.

C. Who can Mentor me?

Many women don't avail themselves of mentoring support because they don't want to impose on others. Unfortunately, this attitude denies the biblical mandate to live in community as interdependent beings. As we receive nurturing from others we are better able to nurture others in return. We are able to give because we have received. And if we refuse to receive, we will soon have nothing to give.

[10] Adapted from "Women's Ways of Mentoring" by Cheryl Dahle, Sept. 1998 http://www.fastcompany.com/magazine/17/womentoring.html

The most essential characteristic of being a mentee is to have a teachable spirit. With a mentor we have the opportunity to gain wisdom, contacts, insights and skill sets that would take us a lifetime to explore on our own. Mentors bring a different perspective to bear as we reflect on our life experiences – turning them into opportunities for learning and growth. And then we are able to do this for others.

When looking for a mentor, first identify your various needs:

- Which of the activities on the chart (Chapter 1) am I looking for a mentor to provide?
- What do I perceive my current home stage of power (Chapter 2) to be and what do I need to develop further?
- Where am I in my faith journey (Chapter 2) and what help do I need to grow in my relationship with God?

Once you have reflected on these questions, then consider who might be the right person for each area in which you wish to develop.

To do this well, think multiple mentors rather than expecting any one person to be able to meet all your mentoring needs. While mentoring is a relationship, it is important to remember that it will seldom be just ONE relationship. Rather, we need to develop a mentoring mentality – a mindset that allows us to learn from anyone. Choose different people to augment the different areas of your life according to the skills, character traits or knowledge you need at this point in your leadership journey.

> ***Successful people turn everyone who can help them into sometime mentors!***
> ***- John C. Crosby, executive director of The Uncommon Individual Foundation***

Some women are looking for someone with whom they can have a strong emotional connection. Others are more interested in the competency of the mentor and therefore comfort isn't important. The reality is that if you look for someone just like you, the potential for discovery is lessened. Instead, look for someone who, by her very nature, will challenge you – whether at a personal or a skills level.

Always go after the very best people and make it easy for them to spend time with you by offering to help them in practical ways – i.e. offer to drive your mentor to work every Friday, pick up her favorite coffee on the way and be punctual; drive her to a speaking engagement and use the travel time to engage in dialogue; go to where she is rather than expecting her to come to you; be creative about finding ways to maximize her time. If a phone call is more realistic – call at a time that works well for her, stick to the agreed upon time frame and follow up with an expression of thanks.

Go for the best – be bold

Treat a mentor like an amazing resource - not someone to be put on a pedestal – and don't expect her to be an expert in all areas.

One way of looking for a mentor is to ask these questions. The answers may give you a hint as to who would be a good mentor for you.

- Who has held up a mirror for me to see something I hadn't seen before?
- Who has given me a nudge in a new direction?
- Who has offered me resources of their life experience, wisdom and lessons learned through their own struggles?
- Who has sponsored me, been a model for me, taught me, discipled me, stood with me through a new responsibility and coached me into confidence?

If these questions don't create a list of possibilities, then follow this plan:

- Be involved in an affirming community.
- Be creative, looking at all the possibilities, starting close to home. List all the people in your sphere of influence. Start with family, friends, colleagues, church family, neighbours, former teachers or professors, people at your gym or volunteer work. The key here is not who you know but who knows the person you need to know.

- Then identify the areas in which you want to be mentored and ask those people for suggestions of people who have the character, credibility and strength in each of those areas.
- Follow-up on those suggestions. Not everyone you ask will agree, or if they say "Yes," will follow through. Don't be discouraged - try again. The results in your life will be worth it! Since mentoring is so important, it is essential to find ways to make it happen.

D. Who can I Mentor?

Mentoring is an investment in others. Therefore the first step is to evaluate what I have to invest. As a potential mentor, I need to be able to give truthful answers to the following questions:

- What are my strengths? Limitations? Gifts?
- What resources can I offer to another? What are my life experiences and what have I learned from those experiences?
- Which of those activities on the chart (Chapter 1) can I do for others?
- What is my primary style? Am I a grace-giver or a truth-teller?
- Where do I see myself on the Stages of Power cycle and/or the Stages of Faith?[11]
- Am I willing to grow along with the one I mentor?
- What am I prepared to offer? Receive?

Having identified your resources, you can begin to look for a mentee.

- Keep alert for unspoken cries for help.
- Issue open-ended invitations.
- Recognize approaches from those who may assume that you are too busy. Questions will be tentative rather than direct.

---

[11] check www.personalpowerproducts.com for on-line assessments

Determine to do some careful preparation. Choose your mentee wisely. You will be investing in her life so look for someone you believe can truly benefit from your input.

Compatibility

A compatible relationship is not essential for the coaching of skills, although it is always an asset. However, compatibility is very important when mentoring involves more personal sharing. It is especially important to have a philosophical compatibility so that your values are not in conflict. If a mentee's goals are incompatible with the values of the mentor, the relationship will flounder. A mentor cannot, with integrity, assist a mentee to develop behaviour, attitudes or skills that are fundamentally contrary to her own belief system.

Caution

Be careful to maintain boundaries. It is seldom wise to enter into counseling or spiritual formation with a friend or to do business with a mentor or mentee.

Use the Assessment Charts on the following pages.

Assessment Chart: Choosing a Mentor

What is my area of need/growth right now? Am I looking for a:

- ☐ Coach
- ☐ Sponsor
- ☐ Teacher
- ☐ Counsellor
- ☐ Discipler
- ☐ Spiritual Guide
- ☐ Model

Is this person someone:	**Yes**	**Don't know**	**No**
who exhibits competence in the area of my need?			
I can trust with this area of my life?			
I can be comfortable with in order to learn from?			
who believes in me and is willing to invest in me?			
who is still learning and growing?			
who will be honest with me?			
who is open and transparent?			
who will help me define my dream?			
who will help turn my dream into reality?			
who will follow my agenda?			
who is able to facilitate learning?			
who has integrity?			
who will celebrate my uniqueness?			
who will challenge me by asking the hard questions?			
who is committed to my success?			

If you cannot answer these questions, plan a conversation in which you will be able to investigate together what the answers would be before you ask for anything specific.

Not every person you seek to mentor you will have all of these characteristics. It is up to you to determine which ones are important to you for each of the areas in which you wish to be mentored.

Assessment Chart: Choosing a Mentee

Is this person someone:	Yes	Don't know	No
in whom I see potential?			
with whom I could easily spend time?			
who is teachable?			
who is comfortable with me – not intimidated by me?			
I can believe in?			
who is self-motivated?			
who is committed to growth?			
who has the discipline to follow through?			
whose values and goals I can fully support?			
is willing to be challenged?			

If you cannot answer these questions, then plan a conversation that will give you an opportunity to ask the kinds of questions that will enable you to answer them before you commit to a longer-term involvement.

An individual may not exhibit all of the characteristics listed. Your role is to determine which of these is important to you and then assess the readiness of a potential mentee to be mentored by you. Look for the level of energy and commitment your mentee is prepared to invest in her own development so that your investment is multiplied in her life.

CHAPTER 4 How?

How is Mentoring Done Effectively?

Once you have agreed to begin a mentoring relationship, the next question is, "How do we proceed?"

This chapter is intended for mentors - to "de-mystify" the process and diffuse fears by giving check lists, tips and practical ideas for each of the steps.

If however, you are the mentee, there is much to learn here that will enhance your learning and growth experience. You can benefit from the understanding, share it with your mentor and be able to ask more specifically for what you need.

Whether you act as sponsor, coach, teacher, discipler, counsellor or spiritual director, there are significant steps to be taken. What differs is the focus of your interaction as well as the length of time and the intensity of that interaction; however, the steps will be similar. (Figure 6)

1. Cultivate a healthy relationship.
2. Create an environment that builds trust.
3. Construct a structure that works for both of you.

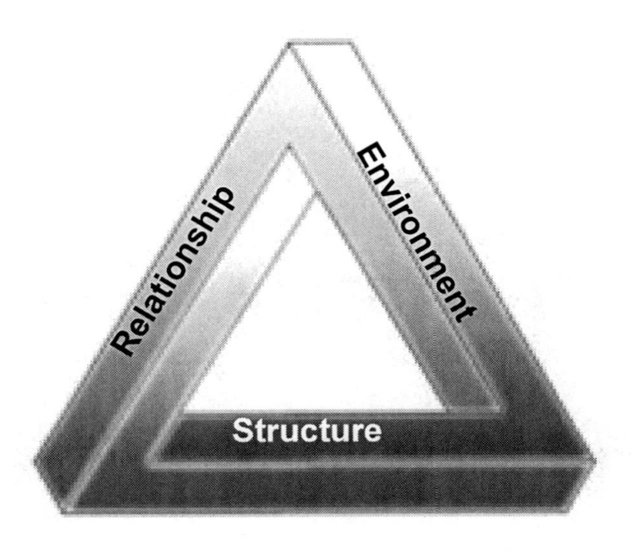

Figure 6

While the steps are communicated here sequentially, they are in reality intertwined. Agreed upon structures help to build an environment of trust, and trust is essential for creating a healthy relationship. Consequently, you don't complete one step and then move on to the next, but rather they are all being built simultaneously.

A. Cultivate a Healthy Relationship

Personal preparation

I have said that mentoring is a

relational process
of
sharing resources
to
empower others.

Healthy relationships are needed for growth to be nurtured and the first step in cultivating healthy relationships is to know yourself. Self awareness is a foundational requirement for building healthy relationships and it requires intentional self-reflection.

Self awareness

As a mentor, it is necessary to see yourself accurately - to know your own strengths and limitations and live out of those without pretence. Only as you understand and accept yourself will you be able to be fully present to another person to listen to their needs, their stories, their struggles and their desire for growth.

We are not able to lead someone beyond where we are in our own development in a particular area. That is as true of faith development as it is of mastering a skill. Scripture tells us:

> *Do not think of yourself more highly that you ought, but rather think of yourself with sober judgment in accordance with the measure of faith God has given you (Romans 12:3).*

We often understand the first part of this verse as a condemnation of pride and move to the other extreme of devaluing ourselves. However, the corollary of thinking too highly of oneself is not to think less of ourselves but to use sober judgment - honest, correct, and well thought through. Paul's admonition is not to be self-deprecating but to have an accurate assessment of ourselves.

Understanding who we are – created in the image of God, gifted by the Spirit, beloved of the Father, redeemed by the Son, destined for glory, called into community – helps us to offer ourselves fully and freely. Understanding our uniqueness in terms of our spiritual gifts and the skills, talents, opportunities and limitations our human heritage and life experience have given us, helps us determine what we have to offer.

There are many inventories to help in the process of self discovery: personality type, stages of faith, stages of power, strengths, learning style, leadership style, spiritual gifts, emotional intelligence, etc. (see appendix 1 for suggestions). The key, however, to the usefulness of those inventories is self reflection. That means asking the same questions of yourself as you would ask of your mentee.

Also, we need both grace-givers and truth-tellers in our lives, but since few people are strong in both, it helps to know our primary style and then recognize the importance of developing the opposite characteristic so that we can communicate truth with grace.

Sodium is an extremely active element found naturally only in combined form; it always links itself to another element. Chlorine, on the other hand, is the poisonous gas that gives bleach its offensive odor. When sodium and chlorine are combined, the result is sodium chloride – table salt - the substance we use to preserve meat and bring out its flavour. Grace and truth can be like sodium and chlorine. Grace without truth can lead us to believe that it doesn't matter what values we adhere to – always taking on someone else's. On the other hand, truth by itself can be harsh and offensive - sometimes even poisonous. Spoken without grace, it can destroy. When truth and grace are combined in a mentoring situation, we are able to preserve and enhance the flavour of life.[12]

In looking for mentors, it is wise to recognize that each mentor will bring a different style to the relationship. To always look for the grace-givers may mean that we don't hear the hard truths that we need to hear. To always look for the truth-tellers may mean that we lack the encouragement we need to make changes. We need the benefit of both styles of interaction.

Questions to ponder

- Who are the people I can look to when I need a listening ear and a good dose of encouragement?
- In what ways am I a grace-giver to myself? To others?
- How can I do this without communicating acceptance of unhealthy behaviours?
- Who are the people in my world that I can trust to tell me the truth?
- What areas in my life need to have a truth-teller?
- How will I intentionally find and nurture truth-telling relationships?
- Am I a truth-teller to myself and others? How can I nurture this ability in a healthy way?

---

[12]Adapted from David H. Johnson.www.esermons.com, Sept. 2003.

Understand the cost and the benefits

As a mentor you can expect:

- to spend time and energy.

  Equipping others is hard work. You will need commitment to see you through. While it is one of the most effective means of developing mature Christians and effective leaders, it is also time consuming.

- to need patience.

  Mentoring is not for the impatient. We live in a culture that wants instant results. But the process of developing character, skills and confidence to act out of core values requires time and maturity which cannot be rushed. Although the process can be assisted and encouraged, there is no such thing as instant fruit. Growth takes time and sometimes comes in spurts.

- to be disappointed at times.

  Mentoring can be discouraging, because people are bound to disappoint you. One of the most difficult things in developing promising leaders is to watch them stop growing. When the potential leader you are developing decides to go no further, remember that you are only called to help them for as long as they are willing to keep growing. When they choose to stop, you can still celebrate their growth to that point - then move on and continue developing others.

- to enjoy a life-time ministry.

  There is real joy in seeing growth and since no one ever outgrows the need for increased character and competency, the need for mentoring continues. Mentoring is a ministry that knows no vocational or organizational boundaries so a mentor is never without a ministry.

  The seemingly slow pace of mentoring is offset by its universal suitability for people of all ages, all races, all nationalities and for all of life.

Personal Preparation Checklist

- Pray for the person you will be mentoring and for the process.
- Know your strengths, your style and your stage of power.
- Be confident enough that you don't have to maintain a façade.
- Reflect on your own life experiences and what they have taught you.
- Plan some initial questions.
- Be prepared to follow the mentee's agenda, not yours.
- Be prepared to listen – to hear her story, to discover her strengths and weaknesses.
- Be willing to meet her where she is in her journey - have realistic expectations.
- Recognize that there is genuine potential for growth but no guarantee.
- Clarify your own expectations of the process and relationship.

First meeting:

Discover your mentee's heart. What is her passion in life? In ministry?

Mentoring requires an investment of time and effort so make sure that your mentee knows what it is going to take. Make sure she understands that you are asking for a commitment to growth and that it is going to stretch her far beyond her comfort zone.

If you are both prepared to proceed:

- Help her to develop an action plan with prioritized goals.
- Choose the goals that you are able and willing to assist in reaching and set a realistic time limit. The time will depend on the goal.
- Establish accountability guidelines.

- Establish frequency of contact, availability, accessibility and boundaries.
- Pray for the Lord to direct your relationship.
- Begin to build trust.

B. Create an Environment that Builds Trust

The single most important factor in building a mentoring relationship is trust.

T Time – to listen and give feedback

R Respect – for the strengths and experience that each person brings

U Unconditional positive regard – acceptance and optimism

S Sensitivity – to each other's feelings, needs and circumstances

T Teachable – both people in the relationship remain open to learning from the other

A safe place for trust to develop so that life transformation can take place requires three things: openness, hospitality, and boundaries. Openness is when you reveal the real you, hospitality is reaching out to embrace another – making a comfortable space for another - and boundaries protect both of you.

Openness

The Johari Window is helpful when considering openness. Think of the quadrants as windows with shades covering them. The open window represents what you know about yourself and what others know about you. That could include your name, occupation, colour of hair, the car you drive, beliefs that you have shared, mannerisms that are obvious, etc. The upper right quadrant represents what others know about you but to which you are blind. You may not know how your voice sounds, how others perceive you or that you have a smudge on your face!! The lower left quadrant represents those things which you know about yourself but have not yet revealed to others such as a painful experience or your favourite food. The lower right corner represents what is unknown both to you and to others. There are certain things known only to God.

Johari Window

	Known to self	Unknown to self
Known to others	*Open*	*Blind*
Unknown to others	*Hidden*	*Unknown*

Figure 7

The process of getting to know another person is one of enlarging the size of the open window. If you begin to pull back the shade covering the hidden window, it increases the open window. As you open up about yourself, you encourage your mentee to do likewise, creating opportunities for input into her life which will decrease her blind area. Then as you ask for feedback from others, you will discover things that will decrease your blind area and will model vulnerability for your mentee.

Enlarging the "Open" Window can be done:

- by sharing your struggles.

  There are two ways to gain wisdom - through your own experience or through the experience of others. Mentors help mentees gain wisdom by sharing their experience. This builds trust, especially when your experience also reveals your failures.

  So don't think that you have to keep up a façade of success. We serve our followers by sharing what did not work as well as what did work. Most of us have learned from our own failures and discovered that it's a lot less painful to learn from the failures of others!

But don't be too quick to share. Your experience is only helpful if it is applicable. Resist the temptation to make the conversation about you by filling in the air with your own stories. Your focus needs to be on the mentee.

- by being real.

  It's not success that causes others to trust – it is being real. This means being honest, open and transparent. It's an issue of integrity.

  We know instinctively when people aren't being sincere and we don't trust them. It's an instinct possessed even by children. So model being real by sharing something of yourself. This generally means taking the risk of exposing some of your own thoughts and feelings, especially ones that often don't get voiced in groups, like fears and anxieties. Don't pretend to be bigger than you are, nor smaller either. Show your humanity, admit when you're wrong or make mistakes. If you don't know something, say so, then do what you can to help find the answers. By taking the risk of being real, you will create an atmosphere of safety.

- by being a learner, too.

  Mentors learn as well as teach. Mentoring relationships are not one-way, hierarchical relationships. While it's true that one has more experience than the other, the "life sharing" goes both ways. Thus, an additional responsibility of a mentor is to accept the mentee's influence. This too builds trust.

Hospitality

I use the term hospitality in its true sense of inviting someone into your life - making space for them - giving them a place to belong - rather than the idea of entertaining.

In biblical times, hospitality was "the process of receiving outsiders and changing them from strangers to guests....Since a stranger lacked legal standing within the visited community, it was imperative that they be under the protection of a patron."[13] This idea beautifully describes the process of mentoring – something quite different from entertaining family and friends. You may begin as strangers, but by welcoming someone into your world, sharing your resources and becoming an advocate or patron for their growth, you move them from stranger to welcome guest.

This kind of "making space for someone" requires an attitude of servanthood. It is shown first of all …

- by respecting and valuing others.

  We show respect by receiving and accepting people for who they are.

  Affirm them. Esteem them. Speak highly of them to others. Encourage them. Instill hope. Appreciate them. Thank them. Recognize their accomplishments.

  People respond to how they are perceived regardless of what you say. They can sense how you see them. When they are valued, they want to be better, try harder, and do the good and right thing.

  Respect and trust is empowering.

- by listening well.

  Trust grows out of the humility of listening well. When a person does not presume to know what's in my head and is willing to hear me out, that engenders trust in me. When people make judgments about what I need without first listening to me, I lose trust in their ability to be helpful. Attentive listening is the key.

  Practice attentive listening with your mentees so that you correctly understand their dreams and fears, their hopes and needs, their challenges and roadblocks.

  Listening well makes it possible for mentors to be like mirrors helping mentees see what's preventing them from being all that

---

[13] Paul J. Achtemeier, editor, *Harper's Bible Dictionary*, Harper and Row, San Francisco, 1985, p. 408

God created them to be. If a mentee's actions or work habits are inconsistent with their stated goals and commitment, the mentor can mention it – not as an attack but as a simple observation. This is when combining truth with grace is important.

We show hospitality when we listen well. What that does is invite someone into a space that is safe and comfortable – a space where they, too, can be real.

- by offering your network.

  Another way of showing your mentee that she is welcome and you are making space for her in your life is by sharing your network! You are in fact bringing her into, and trusting her with, your sphere of influence. That is a vote of confidence.

  Your network consists of the names, postal and e-mail addresses, phone numbers, and personal strengths or interests of people in your formal and informal relationships and, by extension, all the people in their sphere of influence. If your mentee asks about something you don't know about, your immediate response is to consider, "Who do I know who knows something about that?"

  In essence, your network is a crucial portion of your knowledge. We don't have to know it all if we know someone who does! Over the years many of us have built a large network across multiple disciplines. We can create pathways for our mentees by phoning a member of that network on their behalf, by sharing contact information or by arranging a meeting. This is a real indication of trust.

- by offering a safety net for risk taking.

  Mentors often nudge others to take risks that push them outside their previous experience. Although this is uncomfortable at first, it promotes growth and also increases dependence on God. Those who are moving from Stage 2 to Stage 3 especially need the encouragement to take risks. However, at first they may require a safety net – the reassurance that if things begin to fall apart, you will be there to redirect them.

Most people approach any new task - whether parenting or pastoring - with trepidation. Can I even do this? Thus a mentor serves as a confidence builder.

Being committed to your mentee's growth also means being committed to seeing them succeed.

- by praying for them.

  Let your mentee know that you will commit to praying for them and then follow through. Keeping a prayer journal will help.

- by enjoying each other.

  Learn to laugh as well as pray together. Be prepared to see the humour in your own circumstances. Be prepared for the unexpected surprises and celebrate them. Hospitality is simply welcoming someone and enjoying their presence. Have fun.

Boundaries

Boundaries (Figure 8) are necessary to protect both mentor and mentee. Appropriate boundaries can be maintained…

- by clarifying expectations.

  The problem of expecting either too much or too little can be avoided if expectations are discussed openly. Both parties in an effective mentoring relationship need to understand the expectations of the other person. Be clear and specific about what you can offer and don't be afraid to repeat it if other expectations appear. Ask what the mentee's expectations are so that you aren't guessing.

  Everything from "Is there homework?" and "How long do we meet?" to "Who pays for coffee?" should be agreed upon ahead of time so there will be mutual understanding. Unrealistic or unexplored expectations can come back to haunt you later.

  Expectations can be modified as the relationship progresses – but make sure it is by mutual agreement.

- by building in accountability.

  Both mentor and mentee should expect to be accountable to the goals set for the ongoing process. That means appointments kept, promises kept, expectations honoured.

- by assuring confidentiality.

  At the outset mentors and mentees should discuss the kinds of information that would be appropriate to share (1) with anyone, (2) with other mentors, and (3) with each other only. It may take months for mentees to open up, but it takes only a minute to shut them up with inappropriate sharing.

  My rule of thumb for confidentiality is that I only have the right to tell my own story; I do not have the right to tell another person's story unless they specifically request me to do so.

  One mentee, whenever she had a new insight, would declare with enthusiasm, "If there's anyone you think would be helped by hearing my story, please tell them." She meant it, but that permission should never be assumed.

BOUNDARIES and WALLS[14]

HOW TO TELL THE DIFFERENCE

Boundaries	Walls
Define me--who I am, what I think, feel, like or dislike, want or don't want, value, believe, accept and choose, and how I behave and relate.	Obscure who I am, hiding the real me from myself and others so that I and they are not truly aware of what I think, feel, like, dislike, want, need, value, believe, accept, want, or choose.
Encourage me to take responsibility for my thoughts, feelings, choices, actions and attitudes, and hold others responsible for their unfair and hurtful actions as they affect me.	Encourage me to limit my options, feel helpless, and blame others or circumstances for my thoughts, feelings, choices, actions, and attitudes. I have a victim mentality.
Allow me to refuse to let others manipulate, use, abuse or violate me because I respect myself and believe them to be capable of right choices -- motivated by love	Prompt me to deceive, manipulate, use, abuse and violate others to protect myself from what they may do to me -- motivated by fear.
Permit me to say no as well as yes, that is, to make authentic choices.	Decrease my freedom to choose because my fear of others' reactions limits real liberty.
Can be moved in and out by me depending on the other's trustworthiness.	Tend to be maintained rigidly regardless of the other's trustworthiness because I don't trust myself or others.
Allow me to love and be loved.	Keep me from loving and receiving love.
Nurture intimacy.	Prevent intimacy.
Are possible because I am strong.	Are built because I feel weak and helpless to manage relationships well.
Are a sign of health.	Are a sign of dysfunction.
	If another breaches my wall, I have no boundaries behind it to prevent others from taking advantage of me.

Figure 8

[14] Source unknown

C. Create a Structure that Works for Both of You

It is important to create a structure that works for both the mentor and the mentee and is appropriate for the specific focus of the mentoring. A skill may be learned in 6 weeks, but spiritual formation can take years.

Structures can vary

Some mentoring relationships are formal, some informal, some are occasional and some regular, some span a lifetime and some are much more short term.

Some mentees become like another member of the mentor's family. They spend time at their home playing with their children and eating meals. Other times a mentor will simply invite a mentee along on ministry occasions.

Usually mentoring is a one-to-one relationship, but there are other structures that work well. One of the ways in which women have overcome the scarcity of women mentors is to create peer-mentoring circles. They bring together a wealth of experience with the goal of resourcing and encouraging one another. One such network has been developed by Janet Hagberg, the author of *Real Power.* A number of men and women who are prepared to support one another interact via the internet and conference calls, and meet face-to-face once a year to share what each is doing and to find ways of supporting one another. It is a form of peer mentoring, support and accountability to assist each other on their own journey and on projects they have identified.

Another format that could be used is to have a group identify the various areas in which they wish to grow and then have speakers address those topics followed by round-table discussions.

I have also seen value in two mentors who bring different strengths working with one mentee who was transitioning into a new leadership position.

Structure must be designed to serve your goals, so be creative in exploring what works for you.

Meetings can be scheduled or as need arises

If a regularly scheduled meeting is chosen, set a time limit. You may be meeting once a week for 6 weeks or once a month for a year. Whatever you choose, at the end of that agreed-upon time honour your agreement by bringing closure. Then if you both wish to renegotiate another block of time, you are free to do so without feeling obligated. You may plan to stay in touch with occasional updates as a matter of ongoing care.

Some mentors are comfortable with a "call me when you need my input" arrangement rather than a scheduled meeting. That can work well, provided you have set the parameters of when it is appropriate to call (time of day, office or home) and how quickly a meeting can be arranged.

If you have an open arrangement that permits a mentee to call you when the need arises, it is still wise to put a time limit on that. "Call me in the next month if you need help working that through," is wiser than saying, "You may call me anytime." If someone calls you six months later, you may well have forgotten the essence of their concern and it can seem unfeeling. Nevertheless, if that happens, simply ask them to refresh your memory about the details and follow up with clarifying questions.

Have an Agenda

Whatever format is chosen, there are components of the mentoring program that need to be included such as action plans, resources, assignments, deadlines, celebrations and all the other things that go into successful programs including an agenda.

This doesn't mean a formal agenda as you would have for a meeting, but rather that you need to know why you are meeting and what you wish to accomplish.

Mentors are a resource to assist in another's self-directed development. The responsibility for the mentoring relationship, therefore, rests with the mentee not the mentor. This means that the mentoring agenda is driven by the mentee - who should have a fairly clear idea of what she needs and should come to each session with a well-prepared question or two to ask the mentor.

But be flexible enough to recognize teachable moments. Jesus engaged his "mentees" in hours of "debriefing" after healings and miracles and public debates. If mentors encourage mentees to step out into risk-taking adventures, there will be plenty to talk about!

At the beginning of a mentoring relationship, the mentee may not have the knowledge, skills and attitudes to determine their own agenda. They may be expecting the mentor to do the majority of the work. This could be the first "teachable moment" to help them make the shift from thinking that the mentor is the one with authority and control to seeing themselves as the initiator and the mentor as a resource person.

If they come to you without the experience of a previous mentoring relationship, you may be the one to teach them how to take control of their own progress as you clarify expectations, set goals, and plan your structure. Then help them to take on the responsibility as early as possible.

Make use of a variety of tools

- Questions

  One of the most important duties of a good mentor is to ask the right questions. A mentor is not "the answer person," but one who helps develop self-reflection skills since that is what turns an event into a learning experience. Your goal is to move the learner from reflecting *on* the activity to learning *from* the activity.

  Unfortunately, review questions can be understood negatively. The following are some examples of how to make your questions focus on success.[15]

> ***Find the strengths of the student and put them to work, rather than looking at the student as somebody whose deficiencies have to be repaired.***
> ***-Peter F. Drucker***

[15] Roger Greenaway , Reviewing Skills Training, http://reviewing.co.uk

Question asked	Question Heard	Alternative Question
What did you learn?	What did you learn not to do?	What did you achieve? How?
What do you want to achieve?	What can you not do now?	What is your recipe for success? What will you now apply that to?
How can you improve?	What weak points are holding you back?	What strengths can you build on?
What would you do differently next time?	What went wrong this time?	What would you do the same next time?

Sometimes questions identify a deeper issue and it is necessary to bring it to the surface. One of the ways of probing deeper is to ask "why" questions, provided you ask them for information and not in a way that insinuates criticism. If someone tells you that an activity they planned wasn't a success because not many people showed up, you might have the following conversation:

Question asked	Response
Why do you think fewer people came than you hoped for?	Perhaps we didn't advertise enough.
Why do you think the advertising wasn't adequate?	Nobody took on that responsibility?
Why do you think that was?	I guess no one volunteered?
And why do you think no one volunteered?	Perhaps because we didn't list it as a task.

At that point, you can move the discussion into a learning mode by asking, "How do you think you would handle a similar situation another time?

Alternatively, you might take the conversation (and thus the learning) in another direction by asking why the number of people who attended was the chosen measure of success, followed by a clarifying "why?" for each response.

Other times questions lead to personal fears that need to be confronted (see appendix for further questions).

- Signed Covenants

Sometimes mentees need to be held accountable for following through on behaviours they have chosen to adopt and a signed covenant is an effective way of doing so. An example of this might be a leader who has realized that she needs to show her appreciation of her staff in order to build morale.

She might draw up the following covenant.

I, _(mentee)________, have made the commitment to identify one thing that I appreciate about each person on my staff each week for the next month and communicate that to them in a way that they can best receive it.

I covenant with __(mentor)_________to give these messages of appreciation without adding any expectations and I will report the results by___(date)____________.

- Journals

Some of your mentees will already be accustomed to journaling and you can build on that skill by offering specific questions to consider. Others will need to be encouraged to do so. A journal is especially helpful when a mentee becomes discouraged by thinking that no progress is being made. A check through the journal will soon reveal that indeed, progress has been made even if they are just baby steps – and they provide opportunities for celebration.

Journal writing is something that appeals more to some personality types than others. An extravert is someone who processes externally – by talking things through with someone else. She needs to express herself in order to discover what the issues are. This personality type does well with journaling and it is a very helpful tool to develop. On the other hand, an introvert who processes her thoughts internally could not begin to write until she had sorted out in her mind what she wanted to say. To ask an introvert to journal in the standard way would be to impose an unnecessary burden. Instead, the way an introvert can use journaling effectively is to write a one or two sentence summary of her thoughts after a period of self-reflection.

The key is to encourage self-reflection. The tool needs to be adapted to suit the individual. A word of caution here is that your mentee must know that at no time will you ask to read her journal. She is to share only what she wishes.

- Times of Celebration.

Mentoring is mostly about small victories and subtle changes.
-- Marc Freedman, The Kindness of Strangers

Don't wait until the end of your agreed upon time frame to celebrate growth. Find as many ways as possible to celebrate small steps.

Recently, I reviewed with my mentee the goals we had established at the beginning of our relationship. She works from home and found it difficult to keep her work separate from her personal life. She felt that she was working all the time and was discouraged because she didn't think she had made much progress. In the process of reviewing her goals, she was surprised to see the many small steps she HAD made. We celebrated those with gigantic check marks and she left with a sense of accomplishment and with renewed energy to continue to take those small steps.

- Follow-up Strategy

If you have offered your network, check to see if your mentee followed up on it. If homework is one of the agreed upon strategies, or if you have assigned a specific question for journaling, check to make sure it was helpful. Ask what was learned from the process. If you have a covenant agreement, check on the date determined for follow-up.

- Evaluation

One of the expectations to be put in place at the beginning of your mentoring relationships is the need to evaluate the process at specific points. The expectation of evaluation, and a specific time set for it, can be a strong motivator for action and for staying on target for both mentor and mentee.

The word "evaluation" tends to scare most people because it sounds like a pass/fail concept. Evaluation in a mentoring process is not about failing; it is about making the relationship effective for growth. Think of the two of you as a team and then have a mid-point talk about what is going well and what you could change to be more effective as a team. Solicit and provide feedback about your mentoring relationship. Be open to constructive feedback.

Questions for evaluation of the process:

1. What is happening in our time together that you find helpful?
2. What would you like more of?
3. What do you need less of now?
4. What questions do you wish I would ask?
5. What questions do I ask that you think I don't need to?
6. Is the time and structure that we chose still working for you?
7. How have your needs changed since we first met?
8. What changes would be beneficial for the next half of our time together?

Note that your focus for evaluation is on the process of learning, not the person involved. And remember that as a mentor you are not responsible for the outcome, only the input.

CHAPTER 5 When?

When Do I Get Started?

This will be a short chapter because the answer to that question is very short.

The answer is NOW!! Any time! All the time!

There is an urgency for us to fulfill the commands of Scripture to build one another up into full maturity in Christ and so influence our world for God.

Of course, there are preparations to be made. Anything that is worth investing your life in is worth doing well.

Go back through the checklists in the previous chapters, (and find some more in the appendix) - but don't let them be a barrier to investing in someone's life by believing that you need to have a strong and solid "Yes!" beside every characteristic. Instead, use them as the basis for developing your own growth plan and find your own mentor to begin working with you. As you enter into the process yourself, you will be better equipped to assist someone else. Look for someone at a stage or skill ahead of you. Then create a chain – be mentored yourself, mentor someone else and encourage your mentee to also mentor someone.

Then ask God to give you the courage, humility, love, faith and passion to be able to love, serve, teach, confront, affirm and be real.

Mentoring takes:

- courage to be real - vulnerable enough to reveal lessons learned through mistakes - and to confront inconsistencies when needed.
- humility to affirm others' gifts and strengths and to recognize that it is because of the investment of others in our lives that we have anything to offer.
- love in order to communicate acceptance and be willing to serve another.
- faith to be able to believe in the person and the process.
- passion to make a difference in the life of others.

Don't wait. Begin now to be intentional about the legacy that you will leave.

CHAPTER 6

Jesus the Master Mentor

Chapters 1 through 5 have presented the different types of mentoring, the value of mentoring in personal growth, the vision of mentoring others through the stages of power and faith development, the characteristics of an effective mentor, the mechanics of how to mentor, and the urgency of getting started.

There is one more aspect needed to bring all the pieces together into a cohesive whole. That is to look at how Jesus mentored. How did he lead his followers, teach them, disciple them, guide them, walk alongside them in their journey of faith and then release them into ministry?

This will not be a review of the methods Jesus used: parables, metaphors, debriefing after a mission trip, on-site training and so forth. It is possible to grasp all the techniques that we find in the stories and activities of Jesus and totally miss the essence of his interactions with his followers which was all about attitude and values.

At the beginning of his ministry, Jesus was led by the Spirit into the wilderness to be tempted by the enemy - tempted to fulfill his mission in ways that would ultimately compromise the real reason for coming to earth in human form.

I am especially indebted to Henri Nouwen for his book *In the Name of Jesus* which caused me to see the temptations of Jesus with new eyes. I have discovered how the responses of Jesus to the various temptations apply to mentoring.

A Focus on Pleasing People will Compromise Integrity

The first temptation Jesus faced was to become the miracle worker by turning the stones into bread to meet his physical needs. His response was to refuse to allow the immediate needs to take precedence over his ultimate mission and values.

Jesus knew who he was and why he came to earth. His mission was bigger than making people happy by meeting their temporal needs. His role was to reveal the Father and call people to a life of holiness in relationship, first with him, and ultimately with the Father. He knew he could not get sidetracked by the clamour of needs around him which would pull him in all directions.

By choosing to live according to his true identity and purpose, he gave his followers a model of integrity and was able to face every situation and every person in a profoundly real way. Even though miracles were a natural outcome of his compassion and power, he refused to have his identity confined to that one focus.

One of the temptations of being a mentor (especially in Stage 2) is the desire to please our mentees - to make them happy and comfortable - and in doing so, we may sacrifice the greater goal of assisting in their growth.

Its very easy to fall into the trap of thinking that we are to meet every need, but if our highest priority is meeting the needs of others, we will live in response to their call upon our lives rather than according to our internal values.

If we keep our focus on the values that we hold - the motivators in our lives - and clearly articulate them for ourselves, we will be able to remain calm, focused and centered. We will be able to make decisions based on predetermined values and choices. We will be able to see what needs we are called to meet and which ones are outside our jurisdiction or responsibility.

The values and attitudes we embrace become part of us and we naturally live them out. We show love, patience and kindness because those qualities flow out of who we are rather than being a technique we use. And that is the essence of integrity.

Jesus modeled integrity and it was that quality that inspired his followers to stay with him even when they misunderstood his mission. As mentors, we too, must be people of integrity. Then we are to assist our mentees to live out of the internal solid core of their being. They will then give leadership that inspires others to follow them, instead of living a reactionary life in response to external demands and realities.

A Focus on Looking Good will Negate Community and Hospitality

The second temptation Jesus faced was to draw attention to himself by throwing himself from the temple pinnacle and having the angels save him. That would certainly have made him a star attraction that the world would notice, but that was not his reason for being. He came to show us the heart of the Father, to draw us into a relationship with Himself and to create a new covenant community. Living in community requires us to be vulnerable - to be real. That's the choice that Jesus made.

One who is willing to be vulnerable creates an atmosphere of mutuality, respect, and openness. This is true community where the focus is not on self, but on recognizing the input of others where everyone has both value and a voice.

It is in Stage 3 that we develop our abilities and receive recognition for them. It is a necessary step in our development. However, the desire to be the best and draw attention to ourselves can set us apart from others and foster a competitive rather than a cooperative spirit. As a mentor, this defeats the very thing we are trying to do.

Mentoring requires that we focus on our mentees. If we are too engrossed in our own achievements, we will have no time or energy to invest in others. When we seek attention for ourselves we cannot give our full attention to another nor can we serve others wholeheartedly.

In contrast, the willingness to be vulnerable and live in community draws others in - giving them attention and a place to belong.

From every perspective of the world, Jesus came to live among us in the most vulnerable way possible. He took on our humble humanity as a helpless baby to identify with our humanity. He was conceived before marriage which would have brought shame to the entire family. His birth took place among the animals in the unsanitary conditions of a stable. His parents were poor. He lived as a refugee in Egypt. He grew up as a labourer in Nazareth - a place that had a negative reputation ("Nazareth!! Can anything good come from there?" John 1:46). Throughout his earthly ministry he was dependent on others for food and a place to sleep. How vulnerable was all that: socially, emotionally, financially!! And yet when he called followers to him, they gave up their security to become part of his community.

The model he gave us was one of true hospitality, which had nothing to do with house, food and entertainment, but everything to do with his attitude toward people. He shared his heart and his life. He valued, respected, honoured, and served others. He was authentic and vulnerable - embracing them in true community.

As mentors we are called to create a safe place for our mentees to learn to be real, live with integrity and in turn show true hospitality to others.

A Focus on Having Power will Undermine our Mentoring

The third temptation of Jesus was to use the wealth and power of all the kingdoms of the world to fulfill his mission. Jesus' response was to refute the seductive nature of power choosing instead to fulfill his mission by empowering his followers.

Real leaders recognize that they have power but do not need to hold on to it. "They are more concerned about the base they leave upon which others build than they are about the achievements they can claim for themselves."[16]

Jesus left a very good foundation. He invested himself in twelve men and a larger band of men and women who became his followers. He taught them, gave them a vision, prepared them, poured his life into them and gave them a commission. He chose

[16] David McKenna, *Power to Follow Grace to Lead*, Word Publishing, Dallas, 1989, p. 173

them and trusted them. They didn't think they were ready, nor do we, when we consider their human potential, but that small band of men and women turned their world upside down. True, it wasn't in their own strength and power - they were indwelt by the Holy Spirit - but the point is that a true leader and mentor - sees the potential in others, and when they are ready - even if they don't know it - sets them up to carry on.

The desire to hold onto power is a characteristic of Stage 3 leadership and this is the stage where the temptation to use power for self is the strongest - to hold onto power in order to achieve our goals.

But when the pursuit of power becomes our focus, we lose sight of others around us except as people to be controlled in order to maintain our position of power. In our need to control, we lose the ability to trust others. We then don't let go of control and allow others the freedom to act.

The paradox here is that until we give power to others, our achievements are limited to what we can do ourselves. When we empower others, power is multiplied and much more can be accomplished. True leaders function out of an abundance mentality. Power is not limited. Jesus understood this and modeled it for us.

A mentor is someone who is willing to teach others, help them discover their vision, walk and talk with them, trust them to move out and make mistakes, grow and eventually do greater things than they could do themselves - and be able to rejoice in their power.

Laurie Beth Jones in *Jesus CEO* illustrates how Jesus believed in his followers.

> The disciples were constantly arguing over who was the greatest and they dozed off when he needed them the most, yet these were the ones he chose to work with. He visualized the best in them even when there was evidence to the contrary.
>
> He poured a mold of greatness for them and ultimately they went on to fill it...People rise to the occasion when people believe in them. Perhaps we just need someone to show us who we really are

> inside. He said to Simon, "Your name will be Peter and on this rock I will build my church." We all know Peter was impetuous but Jesus saw a solid rock[17]

As mentors, I believe we can give our mentees a vision of who they can be and then hold up that mirror for them to see their own potential. If our mentees are afraid to make mistakes, they'll be afraid to take the risks necessary for growth. They need someone to believe in them. It is only as we genuinely value others for who they are, see their potential and give freely of our resources, that they will be brought to the fullness of maturity in Christ.

A Focus on Integrity, Hospitality and Empowerment is Jesus' Way of Mentoring

Jesus modeled for us the way to mentor others by demonstrating the values and attitudes we need to guide us today.

We live in a world that honours the powerful, the spectacular and the relevant. In fact, most leadership manuals teach you how to achieve one or all of those goals.

As we lead, minister, mentor, teach, coach or disciple others, the temptations of Jesus are common to all of us today: to think that our purpose is to meet everyone's need, to stand out from the crowd by being spectacular in some way and to hold on to the power we believe we need to accomplish our goals.

But Jesus calls us to move beyond pleasing people to living a life of integrity - not seeking to meet everyone's needs but to know our own identity, gifting and call and to live out of that core. Rather than seeking the spotlight for ourselves, we are to exercise hospitality which means drawing others into true community where they are given value and voice. And we are to understand that true power is the power to love, serve and empower others rather than holding onto it ourselves.

---

[17] Laurie Beth Jones, *Jesus CEO.* Hyperion, New York, 1986, p. 197-8

Although he performed many miracles, Jesus was not primarily the miracle worker. Although he attracted attention, that was not his goal. Although he was given all power on earth, he chose to surrender it and die so that the church could be born and be empowered with the eternal power of the Holy Spirit.

Mentoring does not require that we try to please people, be a star or be powerful. Instead it requires us to be people who, like Jesus:

Give a model of integrity
Offer a safe place to belong
Empower others by trusting them

If we do this, we will leave a true legacy in the lives of our mentees, enabling them to do more than we could ever do ourselves.

APPENDIX

Self Discovery Inventories and Resources

Stages of Power	www.janethagberg.com
MBTI	www.humanmetrics.com
	www.psychometrics.com
	www.keirsey.com
Instinct Assessment	www.kolbe.com
Spiritual Gift Assessment	buildingchurch.net/g2s.htm
The Mentoring Group	www.mentoringgroup.com
Values Clarification	www.findingit.com – free e-book

Mentoring Competency Self-Assessment

The following questions are designed to give you a tool for determining where you see the need for increased competency. None of us has "arrived" at the Master Mentor level Jesus modeled for us so this is not to be a discouraging exercise, but an exercise in self awareness. You may wish to ask someone you mentor to help you pull back the shade on the blind area (Johari Window) for your own growth.

Self Mastery

1. I accept myself as I am and seek to be "real" with others.
2. I maintain personal integrity.
3. I fulfill my needs while being honest with others.
4. I am open to feedback, learning and coaching.
5. I manage available time.

Presence - How you present yourself

1. My body language is consistent with my message.
2. I use humour when appropriate.
3. I practice being "here" – in the present moment.

Relating Skills

1. I listen to what is being said and how it's being said.

2. I also listen for what is not being said.
3. I empower others to solve their own problems and process their own issues.
4. I interpret body language and take action to enhance connections.
5. I practice reflective listening so that my mentee is heard and understood.
6. I am empathic. I can put myself in another's shoes.
7. I acknowledge, support and validate others as appropriate.
8. I clarify assumptions to remove barriers to clear communication.
9. I cultivate trust to create a safe environment.

Top 10 Coaching Questions[18]

1. What needs to happen?
2. What's missing?
3. What's getting in the way?
4. What does the ideal outcome look like?
5. What else?
6. What's worked best for you?
7. Can you say more about that?
8. What needs to exist?
9. How will you know when you have it?
10. What are you willing to do?

Getting Acquainted Questions

Use both questions and statements to avoid the other person feeling as if he/she is on the witness stand.[19]

1. I have observed _________. Can you tell me how you learned that?
2. What do you consider to be your best skills?
3. How do you learn best?

---

[18] Sandy Reynolds, Leadership on Purpose, www.leadershiponpurpose.com
[19] The Mentoring Group, www.mentoringgroup.com

4. What is a lesson you have learned through a specific struggle?
5. What is it about that experience that made a difference in your life?
6. Tell me about your mentors.
7. We all leave a legacy. What do you hope yours to be?
8. You mentioned ________________. Tell me more about that.
9. What would make this partnership a valuable experience for you?
10. What might make it a waste of time?
11. How should I refer to you and our relationship when I introduce you to others?
12. Tell me a couple of high points and a couple of challenges in your day/week/month.
    (For high points) What skills, knowledge, or attitudes did you use to help make this happen?
    (For challenges) What part, if any, did you play? Is this part of a larger challenge you're dealing with?
13. Are you open to feedback from me? How would you like it? What should I avoid doing?
14. Describe how you best like to learn.
15. I'd love to hear your story.
16. Tell me some key experiences in your life. What made _____ so important?
17. What do people say you do best?
18. What talents are you most proud of?
19. What makes you laugh?
20. Tell me about some personal accomplishments that you're proud of.
21. What was the best working situation you've ever had?
22. Describe an ideal day for you.
23. What, if anything, would you like to be different in your life?
24. What do you hope your life will look like in one to five years?
25. Describe some key relationships in your life. How have these influenced you?
26. Who are your two most trusted friends? Why?

27. If you could do anything at all, and money were no problem, what would you love to do with your life?
28. What's standing in the way of what you'd like to be or do?
29. Tell me more.
30. What keeps you up at night?
31. What did you feel when you _____?
32. How would your friends/loved-ones describe you?
33. How would your competitors or critics describe you?
34. Tell me about a conflict you had. How did it turn out? What did you do that was effective? What wasn't?
35. How did you decide to _____?
36. May I ask your advice about _____?
37. How do you balance work and the rest of your life?
38. What would you like people to say about you on your _____ birthday? What do you hope they'll forget?

Questions for Developing a Mentee

1. What part of being a mentee/mentor do you like most? Like least?
2. What specific goal do you want to set?
3. How will you know when you reach this goal?
4. On a scale of 1 to 10, what's the likelihood that you'll do what you agreed to do?
5. What's the first step?
6. When will you start?
7. When will you complete it?
8. How could I be a better partner in this relationship?
9. What have I said or done so far that was helpful?
10. What wasn't particularly helpful?
11. I notice that you didn't _____. Is it still a priority?

Questions for a Particular Situation

1. How did this situation begin? Can you share some of the story behind what you're saying (or feeling, or doing)?
2. Tell me what happened next.
3. If you _____, what will probably happen? What would you prefer to happen?
4. What did you feel when you _____?
5. I'm curious about _____.
6. Can you tell me more about that? Give me an example.
7. What if _____ happened?
8. Are there other ways of looking at this issue?
9. Are there ways to make the situation different?
10. What is this situation costing you?
11. How do other people you admire handle similar situations?
12. Where are you now on this?
13. Tell me what you mean by _____.
14. What options do you see? (Help identify several without judging.)
15. What's getting in the way of progress?
16. What do you think should come next?
17. At this point, what matters most to you?
18. Tell me what we can learn from this.
19. As you read/experienced _____, did particular thoughts cross your mind?
20. Describe how this is connected to other events.
21. Is this a pattern of some kind?

More Examples of Alternative Questions

Instead of asking:	Try asking:
What went wrong?	What went right? What were the most promising ideas? Could any of these ideas have worked? If so, how?
What issues shall we put on the agenda?	What issues have shifted down or off the agenda (because they are issues we are dealing with successfully)?
What will you do differently next time?	What will you do the same next time?
What do you need to work on?	What do you have to work with?
What are your needs?	What are your strengths?
What's missing from your team?	Let's do an audit of the talents, qualities and skills already in the team that will help you achieve this next challenge.
What's the problem? How can you fix it?	What's your goal? What are you already doing that will help you get there?
How do you plan to achieve your goal?	In what ways are you already moving towards your goal? What gives you the confidence that you can achieve it?
How did you get into such a mess?	Have you tackled anything like this in the past? What worked then? How can you adapt or build on what worked last time?

Check list
for Making Mentoring Intentional and Effective

	Mentor	Mentee
Cultivate relationships	Follow up on tentative questions about your availability	Follow up on tentative questions about your future
	Issue open ended invitations – then wait	Take the initiative - arrange a coffee or informal talk
	Assess your strengths	Assess your need
	Know your stage of Power/Faith	Look for someone at least one stage ahead of you
	Know your personality type and how it affects communication	Think multiple mentors
	Answer the questions in the Compatibility Chart	
Clarify expectations	Build in accountability and confidentiality	
	Set a specific time frame or specific goal	
	Investigate various structures: one on one, group, peer mentoring, team mentoring? Scheduled or as need arises? Use of journals, signed covenant, times of celebration? Follow-up strategy.	
	Ensure that your communication is understood	Ask for clarification when you don't understand
	Be clear about what you have to offer	Be prepared to communicate what you are looking for
Create an atmosphere of trust and openness	Be real – be human – don't pretend	
	Respect confidentiality	
	Listen well	
	Be patient – recognize that growth takes time and sometimes comes in spurts	
	Establish a structure that works for both of you	

	Mentor	Mentee
	Be ready to invest time and energy	Honour the investment of time – follow through on commitments
	Know your limitations	Don't put your mentor on a pedestal
	Resist the temptation to give answers – ask good questions	Be ready to be challenged to find your own solutions
	Be patient	Be ready to grow
	Share your resources	Use the resources given
	Share your network	Honour the connections
	Follow the mentee's agenda – this is not about me	Have an agenda – this is all about me
	Ask good questions	Expect good questions
	Share your own story, including struggles	Respect the mentor's personal journey
	Build in accountability	Expect to be accountable
	Prepare to be disappointed at times	Take responsibility when you fail to follow through
Conclude well	Recognize that this is but one phase in a lifetime journey	
	Honour the initial time commitment	
	Celebrate milestones	
	Re-negotiate for another specific period of time or another goal if mutually desirable	

BIBLIOGRAPHY

Achtemeier, Paul J. *Harper's Bible Dictionary.* San Francisco, CA: Harper and Row Publishers, 1985.

Biehl, Bobb. *Mentoring: Confidence in Finding a Mentor and Becoming One.* Nashville, TN: Broadman and Holman Publishers, 1996.

Blackaby, Henry and Richard Blackaby. *Spiritual Leadership: Moving People on to God's Agenda.* Nashville, TN: Broadman and Holman, 2001.

Brazelton, Katie. *Conversations on Purpose.* Grand Rapids, MI: Zondervan, 2005.

Buckingham, Marcus. *Now, Discover Your Strengths.* New York, NY: Free Press, 2005.

Elmore, Tim. *Mentoring: How to Invest Your Life in Others.* Atlanta, GA: Equip, 1998.

Flaherty, James. *Coaching: Evoking Excellence in Others.* Burlington, MA: Butterworth Heinemann, 1999.

Jones, Laurie Beth. *The Path.* New York, NY: Hyperion, 1996.

Hagberg, Janet O. *Real Power: Stages of Power in Organizations*, third edition. Salem, WI: Sheffield Publishing Company, 2003.

Hagberg, Janet O and Robert A. Guelich. *The Critical Journey.* Salem, WI: Sheffield Publishing Company, 2003.

Mallison, John. *Mentoring: To Develop Disciples and Leaders.* Adelaide, South Australia: Scripture Union, 1998.

Miller, Jean Baker. *Toward a New Psychology of Women.* Boston, MA: Beacon Press, 1976.

McKenna, David L. *Power to Follow, Grace to Lead.* Dallas, TX: Word Publishing, 1989.

Nouwen, Henri. *In the Name of Jesus.* New York, NY: Crossroad Publishing Company, 2000

Sanders, Martin. *The Power of Mentoring.* Camp Hill, PA: Christian Publishing, 2004.

Stanley, Paul D. and J. Robert Clinton. *Connecting: the Mentoring Relationships You Need to Succeed in Life.* Colorado Springs, CO: NavPress, 1992.

Taylor, Shelley E. and Laura Cousino Klein et al. "Psychological Review" 2000, Vol. 107, No 3. pp 411-429.

Websites Referenced

www.esermons.com

www.fastcompany.com

www.janethagberg.com

www.leadershiponpurpose.com

www.mentoringgroup.com

www.personalpowerproducts.com

http://reviewing.co.uk

Lynn Smith

A school teacher by profession, Lynn served Tyndale University College and Seminary in Toronto, Canada, as Dean of Students and Vice President of Student Development where leadership development became the focus of her involvement with students. The questions of students related to the role of women in the church motivated her to write her first book, *Gender or Giftedness,* which has been translated into a variety of languages.

As a representative of the Evangelical Fellowship of Canada to the World Evangelical Alliance, Lynn connected with many International women. This has resulted in her being asked to speak and teach on the topics of gender, leadership and mentoring in various countries.

The writing of this book on mentoring grew out of her personal involvement with women of all ages who sought her out as an encourager on their personal journey and the request of participants in a weekend leadership conference in Germany to have her teaching notes available for them in book form.

Lynn is married to the Rev. Roger Smith and they are both actively involved as lay-workers in their local church community, Immanuel Baptist Church in Toronto which is affiliated with the Canadian Baptists of Ontario and Quebec.

As one of the founders of NextLEVEL Leadership in 2000, Lynn currently focuses on encouraging Christian women in the marketplace, profession or ministry to develop in the areas of character, competence and confidence in order to have a credible voice and be more effective in their leadership roles in the church and society.

LaVergne, TN USA
22 October 2009
161764LV00003B/1/P

9 780981 046013